GitHub Essentials
Second Edition

Unleash the power of collaborative development workflows
using GitHub

Achilleas Pipinellis

BIRMINGHAM - MUMBAI

GitHub Essentials
Second Edition

Commissioning Editor: Amarabha Banerjee
Acquisition Editor: Noyonika Das
Content Development Editor: Roshan Kumar
Technical Editor: Sushmeeta Jena
Copy Editor: Safis Editing
Project Coordinator: Hardik Bhinde
Proofreader: Safis Editing
Indexer: Pratik Shirodkar
Graphics: Jason Monteiro
Production Coordinator: Aparna Bhagat

First published: September 2015
Second edition: June 2018

Production reference: 1290618

Published by Packt Publishing Ltd.
Livery Place
35 Livery Street
Birmingham
B3 2PB, UK.

ISBN 978-1-78913-833-7

www.packtpub.com

mapt.io

Mapt is an online digital library that gives you full access to over 5,000 books and videos, as well as industry leading tools to help you plan your personal development and advance your career. For more information, please visit our website.

Why subscribe?

- Spend less time learning and more time coding with practical eBooks and Videos from over 4,000 industry professionals

- Improve your learning with Skill Plans built especially for you

- Get a free eBook or video every month

- Mapt is fully searchable

- Copy and paste, print, and bookmark content

PacktPub.com

Did you know that Packt offers eBook versions of every book published, with PDF and ePub files available? You can upgrade to the eBook version at www.PacktPub.com and as a print book customer, you are entitled to a discount on the eBook copy. Get in touch with us at service@packtpub.com for more details.

At www.PacktPub.com, you can also read a collection of free technical articles, sign up for a range of free newsletters, and receive exclusive discounts and offers on Packt books and eBooks.

Contributors

About the author

Achilleas Pipinellis is an open source enthusiast who tries to get involved in as many projects as possible. He was introduced to Linux almost 10 years ago and hasn't looked back since. His distribution of choice is Arch Linux, a lightweight and flexible system that adheres to the KISS philosophy. He likes trying new technologies, especially those that require some sort of special deployment. He also enjoys writing technical guides and articles that help people to learn new stuff and strongly believes that comprehensive documentation is essential to a project's growth and recognition.

About the reviewer

Umesh Ram Sharma has over 9 years, experience in architecture, design, and the development of scalable and distributed cloud-based applications. He has a master's degree in computer science and information technology. He worked as lead developer in companies in the past, and now works as a consultant for various clients. He's an expert in the utilization of the various offers of J2EE, Spring stack, AWS Cloud, MySql, and MongoDB, as well as various open source technologies and libraries.

He's the author of *Practical Microservice* and the reviewer of *GitHub Essentials, first edition.*

> *I would like to thank my family for supporting me in this endeavour; without their support, this would not have been possible.*

Packt is searching for authors like you

If you're interested in becoming an author for Packt, please visit authors.packtpub.com and apply today. We have worked with thousands of developers and tech professionals, just like you, to help them share their insight with the global tech community. You can make a general application, apply for a specific hot topic that we are recruiting an author for, or submit your own idea.

Table of Contents

Preface 1

Chapter 1: Brief Repository Overview and Usage of the Issue Tracker 7
  Exploring the repository's main page 8
    Creating a new repository 8
    The commits page and a comparison with the git log command 11
    The branches page and a comparison with the git branch command 14
    The Raw, Blame, and History buttons 15
    The Watch, Star, and Fork buttons 17
    Changing the description and URL 19
  Learning how to use the powerful benefits of the issue tracker 20
    Creating a new issue 20
    Assigning issues to users 23
    Labels 24
      Why labels are a great asset to UX 25
      Creating new label names and setting different colors 25
      Using labels to group issues 27
    Milestones 28
      Why milestones are a great help when working with code versioning 28
      Creating a new milestone 28
      Adding issues to milestones 30
      Using milestones to see which issues are resolved or are yet to be resolved 30
    Tips and tricks 31
      Learning about the README file 31
      Navigating easily with keyboard shortcuts 31
  Summary 32

Chapter 2: Using the Wiki and Managing Code Versioning 33
  Using the wiki 34
    Why wikis are a nice place to document your project 34
    Creating a new wiki page 34
    Deleting a page 36
    A Markdown-powered wiki – an introduction to Markdown 37
    How to add a sidebar and a footer to your wiki 40
    Watching a wiki page's commit history and reverting to a previous state if needed 42
  Managing code versioning 46
    Creating a release 47
    Editing a release 50
    Pushing a tag from the command line 51
    Marking as pre-release 51

Making a draft of a release   53
Uploading your own files   53
Tips and tricks   54
Subscribing to new releases via atom feed   54
Editing the wiki locally   55
Installing gollum   55
Cloning the wiki and viewing the preview in your browser   55
Making changes locally and pushing to GitHub   56
Summary   57
Chapter 3: Managing Organizations and Teams   59
The difference between users and organizations   60
Organization roles and repository permission levels   60
Creating an organization   61
Global member privileges   64
Repositories   66
**Teams – a great way to grant selective access to your organization
projects**   67
Creating a team   67
Inviting people   69
Accepting an invitation   71
Team member permissions   72
Requesting to join a team   73
Step one – as a user   73
Step two – as an owner or team maintainer   73
Adding repositories to a team   74
Team discussions   76
The People tab   77
Managing access levels   78
Difference between Members and Outside collaborators   80
Demoting to an outside collaborator   83
Organization settings   83
Profile   84
Security   85
Audit log   85
Third-party access   86
Teams   86
Tips and tricks   86
How to transfer a repository to an organization's namespace   86
How to convert a user account into an organization   89
Mentioning teams   89
Organization feed only in dashboard   90
Summary   91
Chapter 4: Collaboration Using the GitHub Workflow   93

Learning about pull requests 93
Why pull requests are a powerful asset to work with 94
The connection between branches and pull requests 94
Creating branches directly in a project – the shared repository model 95
Creating branches in your fork – the fork and pull model 95
How to create and submit a pull request 95
Using the Compare & pull request button 95
Using the compare function directly 98
Using the GitHub web editor 100
The shared repository model 101
The fork and pull model 102
Submitting a pull request 104
Peer review and inline comments 105
The layout of a pull request 106
The review process 110
Correcting mistakes 114
Merging the pull request 115
Removing/restoring a branch after the pull request is merged 116
Reverting a pull request 117
Tips and tricks 117
Closing issues via commit messages 117
Task lists in pull requests 119
Downloading the diff of pull requests 121
A global list of your open pull requests 121
Adding a LICENSE file using the web editor 121
Creating new directories using the web editor 122
Summary 123
Chapter 5: GitHub Pages and Web Analytics 125
GitHub Pages 125
Creating a user or an organization page 126
Creating a project page 126
Choosing a theme to style your page 127
Using a custom domain 129
Introducing Jekyll 130
Installing Jekyll 130
Customizing your page using Jekyll 131
Read more about Jekyll 133
Web analytics 134
Pulse 134
Contributors – additions/deletions 135
Community profile 136
Commits over time 138
Code frequency 139
Dependency graph 140
Network 140

Forks	142
Traffic	142
Tips and tricks	143
Making use of Github Pages' metadata with Jekyll	144
Summary	145
Chapter 6: Exploring the User and Repository Settings	147
User settings	148
Profile	150
Setting up multiple emails	150
Managing your SSH keys	152
Setting up two-factor authentication	153
Repository settings	154
Changing the default branch that appears in a repository's main page	154
Enabling/disabling the wiki	155
Enabling/disabling the issue tracker	156
Adding collaborators	156
Transferring ownership – user to organization	157
Deleting a repository	158
Tips and tricks	158
Finding the size of your repositories	158
Fine-tuning email notifications	159
Summary	159
Other Books You May Enjoy	161
Index	165

Preface

GitHub is the leading code-hosting platform with literally millions of open source projects having their code hosted on it. In conjunction with Git, it provides the means for a productive development workflow and is the preferred tool among developers.

Starting with the basics of creating a repository, you will then learn how to manage the issue tracker, where your project can be discussed. Continuing our journey, we will explore how to use the wiki and write rich documentation that will accompany your project. Organization and team management will be the next stop, and then the pull requests, which made GitHub so well known.

Next, we will focus on creating simple web pages hosted on GitHub, and, lastly, we will explore the settings that are configurable for a user and a repository.

Who this book is for

This book is intended for experienced or novice developers with a basic knowledge of Git. If you ever wanted to learn how big projects such as Twitter, Google, or even GitHub, collaborate on code, then this book is for you.

What this book covers

Chapter 1, *Brief Repository Overview and Usage of the Issue Tracker*, explains some of the main features GitHub provides and what you can make out of them. The issue tracker is the heart of communication between a project's developers and/or users. Consider it to be a notepad dedicated to each repository where you track bugs, reports, feature requests, and anything else that can be written down. GitHub has implemented many other features that sit on top of the issue tracker, such as labels and milestones, which provide the ability to better visualize and categorize all the issues.

Chapter 2, *Using the Wiki and Managing Code Versioning*, helps you learn how to create, edit, and maintain a wiki by providing a home for your documentation that will complement your project. You will also learn how to create a new release out of an existing branch or tag, accompanied by optional release notes. In this way, the end user can understand the changes from any previous versions.

Chapter 3, *Managing Organizations and Teams*, teaches you how to create and manage the organizations that you are the owner of. You will also learn how to create teams, add users to them, and assign different access levels according to your needs.

Chapter 4, *Collaboration Using the GitHub Workflow*, focuses on how to work with branches and pull requests, the most powerful features of GitHub.

Chapter 5, *GitHub Pages and Web Analytics*, takes you through how to build web pages around your project, hosted exclusively on GitHub. You have the ability to make static web pages using HTML, CSS, and JavaScript.

Chapter 6, *Exploring the User and Repository Settings*, explores the most common and essential settings of a user and a repository. As a user, there is a lot of information you can set up in your user settings page, such as associating more than one email to your account, adding multiple SSH keys, or setting up two-factor authentication. Similarly, some functionalities of a repository can be set up via its settings page. For example, you can enable or disable the wiki pages and grant write access to the public, or completely disable the issue tracker.

To get the most out of this book

For this book, you'll need Git (any version will do) and a GitHub account.

Download the example code files

You can download the example code files for this book from your account at www.packtpub.com. If you purchased this book elsewhere, you can visit www.packtpub.com/support and register to have the files emailed directly to you.

You can download the code files by following these steps:

1. Log in or register at www.packtpub.com.
2. Select the **SUPPORT** tab.
3. Click on **Code Downloads & Errata**.
4. Enter the name of the book in the **Search** box and follow the on screen instructions.

Once the file is downloaded, please make sure that you unzip or extract the folder using the latest version of:

- WinRAR/7-Zip for Windows
- Zipeg/iZip/UnRarX for Mac
- 7-Zip/PeaZip for Linux

The code bundle for the book is also hosted on GitHub at `https://github.com/PacktPublishing/GitHub-Essentials-Second-Edition`. In case there's an update to the code, it will be updated on the existing GitHub repository.

We also have other code bundles from our rich catalog of books and videos available at `https://github.com/PacktPublishing/`. Check them out!

Download the color images

We also provide a PDF file that has color images of the screenshots/diagrams used in this book. You can download it here: `http://www.packtpub.com/sites/default/files/downloads/GitHubEssentialsSecondEdition_ColorImages.pdf`.

Conventions used

There are a number of text conventions used throughout this book.

`CodeInText`: Indicates code words in text, database table names, folder names, filenames, file extensions, pathnames, dummy URLs, user input, and Twitter handles. Here is an example: "Mount the downloaded `WebStorm-10*.dmg` disk image file as another disk in your system."

A block of code is set as follows:

```
echo "\n## Description\n\nGitHub for dummies" >> README.md
git add README.md
git commit -m "Add second level header to README file"
git push origin add_description
```

When we wish to draw your attention to a particular part of a code block, the relevant lines or items are set in bold:

```
echo "\n## Description\n\nGitHub for dummies" >> README.md
git add README.md
git commit -m "Add second level header to README file"
git push origin add_description
```

Any command-line input or output is written as follows:

```
mkdir -p ~/github-essentials
cd $_
```

Bold: Indicates a new term, an important word, or words that you see onscreen. For example, words in menus or dialog boxes appear in the text like this. Here is an example: "Select **System info** from the **Administration** panel."

Warnings or important notes appear like this.

Tips and tricks appear like this.

Get in touch

Feedback from our readers is always welcome.

General feedback: Email feedback@packtpub.com and mention the book title in the subject of your message. If you have questions about any aspect of this book, please email us at questions@packtpub.com.

Errata: Although we have taken every care to ensure the accuracy of our content, mistakes do happen. If you have found a mistake in this book, we would be grateful if you would report this to us. Please visit www.packtpub.com/submit-errata, selecting your book, clicking on the Errata Submission Form link, and entering the details.

Piracy: If you come across any illegal copies of our works in any form on the Internet, we would be grateful if you would provide us with the location address or website name. Please contact us at copyright@packtpub.com with a link to the material.

If you are interested in becoming an author: If there is a topic that you have expertise in and you are interested in either writing or contributing to a book, please visit authors.packtpub.com.

Reviews

Please leave a review. Once you have read and used this book, why not leave a review on the site that you purchased it from? Potential readers can then see and use your unbiased opinion to make purchase decisions, we at Packt can understand what you think about our products, and our authors can see your feedback on their book. Thank you!

For more information about Packt, please visit `packtpub.com`.

Brief Repository Overview and Usage of the Issue Tracker
1

Almost everything that happens on GitHub happens in the context of the repository. A repository is like a folder that contains all the files of your project.

The landing page of a repository on GitHub depicts the content of a person's local Git repository. Apart from the tree-like structure of the files, GitHub also provides some additional features that bring the most well-known and frequently used Git commands to your browser. Among others, these include the branches, commits, and tags of your repository.

In addition to these features, GitHub also provides an issue tracker for each repository. This is where the discussions take place, bugs are tracked and reported, features are requested, and pretty much anything else that is relevant to the project is discussed.

GitHub has also implemented many other features that sit on top of the issue tracker, such as labels and milestones that provide the better visualization and categorization of issues. We will explore all the features extensively, so don't worry if you aren't familiar with these terms yet. Here's what we'll cover in this chapter:

- Exploring the repository's main page

- Learning how to use the powerful benefits of the issue tracker

 The terms **project** and **repository**, although not the same thing, will be considered to have equal meaning, and will be used interchangeably throughout this book.

Exploring the repository's main page

The main page of a repository is the place where people spend most of their time when visiting a project. In this section, you will learn how to create a repository, and then we will explore the vast features of GitHub that bring Git's command line to your browser.

Creating a new repository

Assuming you have already signed up to GitHub through `https://github.com/join`, we will now explore the main repository's page and learn how to create a new repository that will host your code.

Navigate to the top-right of the page, click on the little cross beside your username, and choose **New repository**, as shown in the following screenshot:

You will then be taken to a page where you need to provide some information about your new repository:

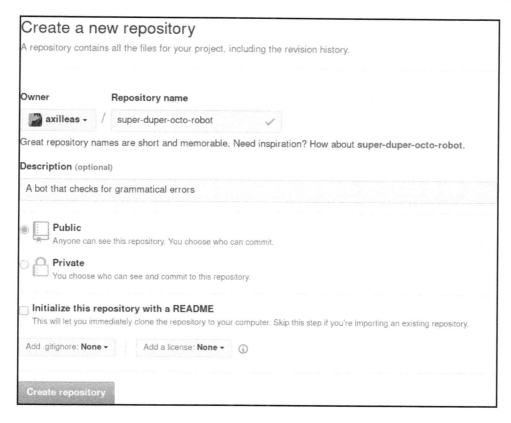

Fill in a name under **Repository name**, which will ultimately form the URL under which your repository will be registered. This is the minimum action you need to perform in order to create a repository.

> All the repositories on GitHub have the following URL scheme:
> `https://github.com/<username>/<repository_name>`

It is optional, but recommended, for you to provide a description for your repository. That way, other users can tell at a glance what your project is all about.

The next setting to choose is whether your repository will be **Public** or **Private**. Generally, you go with public, unless you do not want your files to be seen by everybody. However, the private repositories come with a price.

The very next thing GitHub provides is the ability to create the repository with a README file. Readme files usually include comprehensive information about the project you are hosting under your repository, such as installation guides, and build and usage instructions, as well as guidelines on how you can contribute. You can always add a README file later, so leave this option unchecked for the time being.

Another nice feature is the ability to choose and include a gitignore file upon creation. You can choose from a collection of the useful .gitignore templates taken from https:// github.com/github/gitignore.

Ultimately, the code that you will host on GitHub will be able to be forked and reused by third parties. If you are starting a fresh, new repository, you can choose a license to include upon creation. Again, this is optional, and you can always manually add a license file later.

Let's hit the **Create repository** button and finish the repository creation. Here's what it looks like so far:

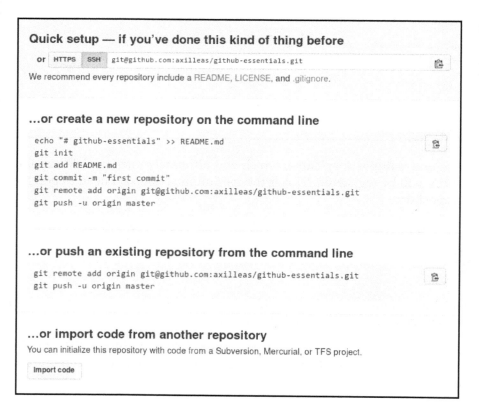

You can see that GitHub provides useful information on what to do next. If you already have an existing Git repository locally on your computer, you can push its code to GitHub or start fresh by following the on-screen instructions.

 Since we will be working from the command line later, it is highly recommended that you generate an SSH key to use with your GitHub account. Follow the guide at `https://help.github.com/articles/generating-ssh-keys/`. Also, make sure that you properly configure your Git username and email settings. For more information, see `https://help.github.com/articles/setting-your-username-in-git/` and `https://help.github.com/articles/setting-your-email-in-git/`.

Congratulations on creating your first repository!

The next goal is to explore the repository's main page. This is the page you see when you navigate to `https://github.com/<username>/<repository>`, where you should see the following:

- `<username>`: This is the username you registered with (found in the top-right corner)
- `<repository>`: This is the **Repository name** you entered in the previous steps

The commits page and a comparison with the git log command

GitHub has a nice web UI that many common `git` commands can be entered in.

Let's first create a `README.md` file and push it to GitHub in order to explore the commits page:

1. Create the directory that will hold your code and `cd` into it:

```
mkdir -p ~/github-essentials
cd $_
```

2. Then, follow GitHub's instructions on creating a new project:

```
echo "# github-essentials-v2" >> README.md
git init
git add README.md
git commit -m "first commit"
git remote add origin git@github.com:<username>/<repository>.git
git push -u origin master
```

Note that I use the Git protocol (https://github.com/) that uses SSH underneath, so I don't have to type my username and password each time (see the previous note on how to achieve this).

 The directory name (in our example, github-essentials) could be totally different from the repository name you entered upon creation. It is the remote URL you set with git remote add that must match with the repository URL GitHub provides.

Every time you add more commits, their total number will also appear on the project's main page. In the preceding steps, we did our first commit, so the count is set to one, hence the **1 commit** option shown in the following screenshot:

Click on the **1 commit** link as shown in the preceding screenshot to enter the commits page.

From here, you can browse the list of commits (so far, we only have one) and visualize the output of git log. Let's compare those two commits. Type git log in your local repository; the output should be similar to the following:

```
commit b77a7ff22653ca74b10e99efdbc45f6f54ef10f4
Author: Achilleas Pipinellis <mail@example.com>
Date:   Sun Apr 15 23:26:32 2018 +0200

    first commit
```

Now, head over to the commits page on GitHub. Here, you can see the same information depicted in a nice interface:

We can see the commit message and the date and time it was committed, as well as the SHA of the commit. Note that the SHA is stripped down to the first 7 characters out of 40. Clicking on either the SHA or the commit message will show the changes introduced by that specific commit. Let's do that and compare what GitHub shows for the `git show <commit>` command:

```
commit b77a7ff22653ca74b10e99efdbc45f6f54ef10f4
Author: Achilleas Pipinellis <mail@example.com>
Date:    Sun Apr 15 23:26:32 2018 +0200

    first commit

diff --git a/README.md b/README.md
new file mode 100644
index 0000000..54a8290
--- /dev/null
+++ b/README.md
@@ -0,0 +1 @@
+# github-essentials-v2
```

The result of the preceding code is shown in the following screenshot:

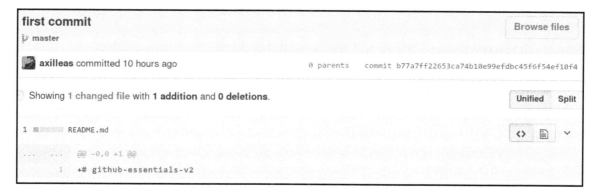

The commit message is shown in big bold letters, since it conveys an important message. Right under it, there are the branches where the commit is included (currently, it is only **master**).

You can see the commit SHA, the author name, and the date right under the blue area. GitHub also tells you how many files changed during the last commit and how many additions/deletions were made during that commit.

Lastly, we can see the added changes in green. If, instead, you remove something, it will be shown in a pinkish color, as we will see later on.

The branches page and a comparison with the git branch command

Let's create a branch named add_description and checkout into it:

```
git checkout -b add_description
```

Next, edit README.md, add some text, make a new commit, and push it to GitHub:

```
echo "\n## Description\n\nGitHub for dummies" >> README.md
git add README.md
git commit -m "Add second level header to README file"
git push origin add_description
```

Now let's create a second branch named new_feature out of the master branch and just push it to GitHub:

```
git checkout master
git branch new_feature
git push origin new_feature
```

Now its time to switch to GitHub and see how all this information is presented.

In the main repository page, you can now see that there are three branches. Click on the **branch** link to get more information.

The **Overview** page is, as the title suggests, an overview of the other tabs you see next to it. It tells us what the default branch is, what branches you have pushed from your account (same as the **Yours** tab), and the most active branches in the last three months, sorted by date (same as the **Active** tab). The **Stale** tab represents the branches that haven't been updated for more than three months.

You can change the default branch that appears on your project's homepage in the project's settings. This is covered in detail in Chapter 6, *Exploring the User and Repository Settings*.

You may notice that although we pushed the **new_feature** branch after we pushed **add_description**, its update time appears to be before **add_description**. This is only natural, since **new_feature** has the same commit date as our master branch, which is dated before the **add_description** branch.

Now, if you look closely at the tab where the branches are shown, you can see, written in a small font, the number of commits that the branches are behind or ahead of the default branch by—in our case, the default branch is **master**.

From the branches page, you can delete all the branches, except for the one you have set as default. Let's try and delete the **new_feature** branch. Click on the red trash icon and watch what happens. GitHub gives you the chance to restore a recently deleted branch:

new_feature   Deleted just now by axilleas   **Restore**

 If you refresh the page or browse in another area of the page where you deleted the branch, the **Restore** button will disappear.

The **New pull request** button will be explored in a different chapter.

The Raw, Blame, and History buttons

Now that we have explored how GitHub sees branches, let's take a look at some other Git functionalities that GitHub provides.

The **Raw, Blame,** and **History** buttons appear when viewing a single file of a repository. For example, let's visit the README.md file by clicking on it:

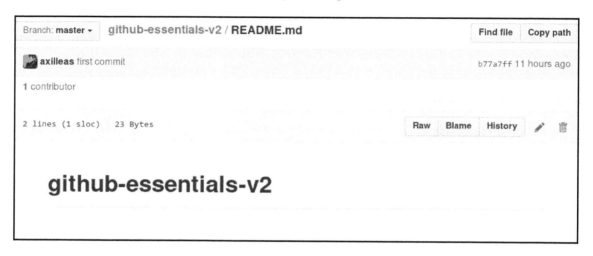

The **Raw** button, like the name suggests, opens the file in a raw form, meaning that any HTML formatting disappears. This is particularly useful when you want to download a single file. You will notice that many guides on the internet use this raw file format when they tell you to download something using command-line tools, such as wget or curl. If you have ever tried to download a file from GitHub and all you got was an HTML file, remember the usage of raw.

The **Blame** button makes use of Git's blame function. Basically, for each line of a file, Git informs you about who modified that line and when that line was modified. If you want to know more, visit https://git-scm.com/docs/git-blame.

In order to properly see how that works, I will not use our previously created README.md file, since there is not much information there to see how GitHub uses this Git function. Instead, I will use a file from another repository with more commits. Take, for example, https://github.com/gitlabhq/gitlabhq/blame/master/app/models/ability.rb, as shown in the following screenshot:

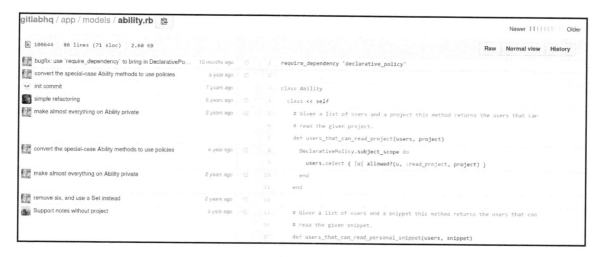

Downloading the example code

Compared to invoking `git blame` in the terminal, you can feel the superiority of GitHub's feature. Every line of code is annotated so you can see when and what commit changed a particular line of the file and who changed it. There is also the nice little feature of hotness: Older commits get a brown line whereas newer ones are colored yellow.

Finally, the **History** button is nothing more than what `git log` does for a particular file.

The Watch, Star, and Fork buttons

You've probably spotted the three buttons sitting at the top-right corner of your repository page. These appear for every public repository, not only your own.

The **Watch** button manages the level of subscription in a repository. GitHub notifies you with an email whenever an action takes place in a repository you follow and, at the same time, it lists them in the **Notifications** area (`https://github.com/notifications`) where you can later mark them as read, as shown in the following screenshot:

There are three levels of subscription, ranging from "never be notified" to "Big Brother". You can choose to be notified only if you explicitly take part in a conversation or if someone mentions you (**Not watching**). This is the mid level of notification you can get, and is the default behavior when you create a new repository. The next level is to always be notified, for example, whenever a conversation begins, or a new issue is created, or someone leaves a comment in a line of code, or someone mentions you (**Watching**). Finally, the third option is to never be notified (**Ignoring**).

You can mention someone by prefixing their username with the *at* sign (@). This is the special way in which GitHub can understand that you need someone's attention. Start typing the username and GitHub will be smart enough to autocomplete it.

The **Star** button is a way to show your appreciation to a repository and its creator. It depicts the popularity of a project. Whenever you star a repository, it gets added to your list of starred repositories. You can see all your starred repositories at `https://github.com/stars`.

A list with the most starred projects on GitHub can be found at `https://github.com/search?utf8=%E2%9C%93q=stars%3A%3E1type=Repositories`.

You can see the people who have starred a repository by clicking the number next to the **Star/Unstar** button. For the repository I just created, you can see that I am the only stargazer:

The **Fork** button and its purpose is what made GitHub excel in the first place. As we will see later in this book, its main use is when you wants to contribute to a project. When you fork a repository, it gets copied in your own namespace, and that way you have full ownership of that copy; thus, you are able to modify anything you want. Go ahead and try it. Go to https://github.com/axilleas/github-essentials and press the **Fork** button. After a short while (depending on the size of the repository), you will be redirected to your own copy of this repository that you fully own.

Changing the description and URL

Previously, we learned how to add a description to our project. This was optional when creating a new repository, so if you opted out of creating it, let's see how to add it now.

Head over to the main repository page. You will be presented with two blank forms. In the **Description** field, put a descriptive note of your project; in **Website**, put the website URL that your project might have. This could also be your GitHub repository's URL. Here's what it looks like:

After you hit **Save**, you will immediately see the changes.

Learning how to use the powerful benefits of the issue tracker

GitHub provides a fully featured issue tracker, tightly tied to each repository.

Its primary use is that of a bug tracker, since reporting and discussing bugs play a vital role in the growth of your project. It can also be used to make feature requests, serve as a discussion board of a blog or a project, and even be used as a notepad for repairing your house! For this, you can refer to the following links:

- http://github.com/andreareginato/betterspecs/issues
- https://github.com/frabcus/house/issues

Creating a new issue

Go to https://github.com/<username>/<repository>/issues for an overview of all issue activity. If no one has ever opened an issue in your project, you will be presented with a blank page with GitHub prompting you to open a new issue. Let's go ahead and do this. Click on the big green button that says **New issue**.

An issue can be created when you provide the minimum of a title. Look at the following screenshot carefully where the **Submit new issue** button is grayed out and cannot be clicked. The title should be as descriptive as possible of the message you are trying to pass when creating an issue.

Below, under the **Write** tab, you can provide the details and essentially start a discussion with everyone who wants to participate (if the repository is public, that is). That's why GitHub cleverly suggests to **Leave a comment**.

Besides writing, you can also attach images by simply dragging and dropping, or by selecting them using folder navigation. Here's what the very first issue of this repository looks like:

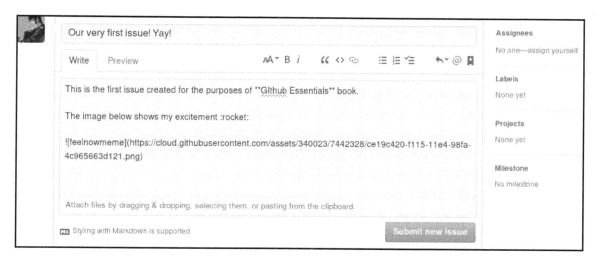

Next to the **Write** tab is the **Preview** tab. In order to understand its purpose, you must first learn about Markdown.

In brief, Markdown is a text-to-HTML conversion tool so that you can write text that contains structural information and then automatically convert it to valid HTML. Written by John Gruber and adopted by GitHub (among many others), Markdown is the most well-known text-to-HTML conversion tool because of its ease of use.

 You can read all about how GitHub extends Markdown's functionality in the guide available at `https://guides.github.com/features/mastering-markdown/`.

Now, back to our new issue. As the name suggests, **Preview** shows what the result will be when you submit the issue. It will style the regular text of the **Write** tab into a meaningful text accordingly, with URLs properly formatted, images shown, emojis displayed, and so on.

 As we will see later in this book, GitHub-flavored Markdown has many little gems that leverage the usage of the issue tracker. What you have seen here is just the tip of the iceberg.

Feeling ready to submit it? Hit **Submit new issue** at the bottom of the page. Congratulations on making your first issue! The result will look as follows:

Each created issue is assigned a unique number that we can later use in other issues for reference. In our example, since this was the very first issue, it was assigned the number #1. Some useful information is provided in the title area. You can see that the issue is marked as **Open**, the username of the person who created it, the time it was created, and how many comments there are.

If you later realize that you made a mistake, don't panic—you can always edit the issue you created. The **Edit** button allows you to edit the title, and the pencil icon is used for editing the description. Close the issues using the **Close issue** button.

You can comment and close the issue at the same time if, for example, you also want to leave a note as to why the issue got closed. Start typing a comment and the button will change from **Close issue** to **Close and comment**.

Assigning issues to users

A repository can have more than one collaborator. A collaborator is a person who has push access to the repository and, in our case, can also edit and close issues.

User assignment works well in repositories with large traffic where a team is involved and is responsible for bug fixes, enhancements, and so on.

There are two ways to assign an issue to someone. First, as you have seen in the previous images, there is an **Assignee** section inside each issue, as shown in the following screenshot:

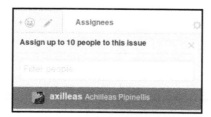

At this particular stage, there is only one collaborator—me—so only my name appears in the list. Okay, we learned how to assign an issue to a collaborator from inside the issue, but what happens if you have dozens of issues that you want to assign to someone? Assigning each of them one by one is a bit tedious and time consuming. You'll be happy to know that you can mass-assign issues to a person.

For this purpose, let's create two more issues. Head over to the **Issues** page, select the boxes of the issues that you want to assign, and select an assignee, as shown in the following screenshot:

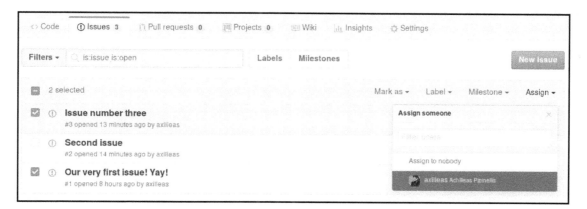

After selecting the assignee, the issues will immediately get updated with the new information. You can see that the avatar of the assignee appears on each issue that is assigned to them:

 You can select and add up to 10 assignees to an issue.

Labels

If you have worked with WordPress, labels are like tags. This is not to be confused with Git tags, though. We will now explore how to create labels and use them effectively to easily categorize batches of issues.

Why labels are a great asset to UX

Labels provide an easy way to categorize the issues based on descriptive titles, such as **bug**, **feature**, and any other words you feel like using. They are colored, and are visible throughout the issue tracker or inside each issue individually.

With labels, you can navigate to the issue tracker and filter any bloated information to visualize only the issues you are interested in. Let's see how that works.

Creating new label names and setting different colors

Head over to the issue tracker and navigate to the label page by clicking on **Labels**. As you can see, GitHub sets up some predefined labels that are ready to use. The name, color, and description are fully customizable for new and existing labels.

Creating a new label is as easy as pressing the **New label** button, filling in the name, choosing a color, and optionally entering a description. In fact, a random color is already picked, so the only prerequisite is the name. I have created a new yellow label named `needs testing`, as shown in the following screenshot:

After clicking the **Create label** button, the label will be created and appear in the list. Back to the issues—let's go inside the first one and give it the label we just created. Click on the gear icon for the dropdown to appear. Start typing to narrow down the search. Now, we only have 9 labels, but imagine having more than 42. You'd have to scroll and scroll until you found the label you were looking for.

As you might have guessed, you can choose more than one label in an issue. After you choose them, just click anywhere outside of the label window to save the action. You will see the changes immediately:

Note how GitHub makes note of any change made to the issue. This way, you will know who took a specific action and when the action was taken. Nothing escapes GitHub's eye! Try to remove the enhancement label to see what happens.

As with the assignees, you can also mass-assign labels to issues. Let's try this by going to the main issues page and selecting some issues, and then choosing the **bug** label:

The issue tracker will be updated, and now you can have an overview of the issues with the labels assigned to them:

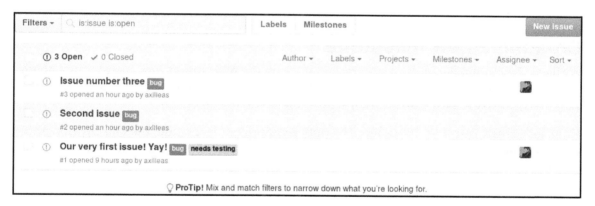

Using labels to group issues

Suppose you have 100 opened issues, many labeled as bugs. Wouldn't it be cool if somehow, only those issues appeared in the **Issues** main page? Well guess what—when you click on the **bug** label, GitHub basically makes a query and, as a result, only the **bug** issues appear. Grouping to the rescue!

Going back to the **Labels** page, you can see that you can have an overview of the number of issues assigned to each label.

Milestones

Milestones, much like labels, are primarily used to group issues, but for different purposes. Consider a milestone such as a special label that has a title, a description, and an optional due date.

Why milestones are a great help when working with code versioning

It is common knowledge that applications are released in versions. From the BIOS of your laptop to the web browser you use to explore the internet, all applications use versioning.

Many companies, or even community-driven, open source projects, tend to have a road map that dictates the time when the new product will be released to the public.

GitHub integrates this feature with the issue tracker. Let's dive in and learn how to create a new milestone, attach some issues to it, and use the overview to see what issues remain resolved or unresolved.

Creating a new milestone

While at the main page of the issue tracker, click on the **Milestones** link, next to the **Labels** link. If no milestone has been created yet, you have two buttons that can create a milestone. Generally, the **New milestone** button will be the main one to use.

Now, let's create our first milestone. The only requirement is the title; the **Description** and **Due Date** fields are optional. However, just to see what it looks like, let's add all the information:

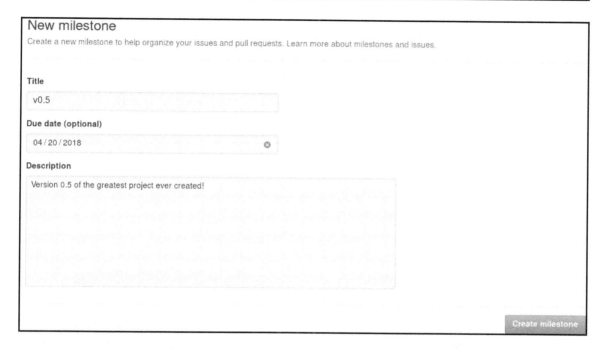

Hit **Create milestone** and it will appear in the **Milestones** page with all the information we previously entered:

On the left-hand side, there is the name, the due date, the description, and a note of the time the milestone was last updated. On the right-hand side, you can see the percentage of completion and the number of open and closed issues. Of course, you can edit, close, or delete it completely.

Adding issues to milestones

Now that we have at least one milestone, let's set it to an issue.

Again, there are two ways to add a milestone to an issue. Much like assignees and labels, you can do this inside each issue or mass-add it when in the **Issues** main page. Here, I will try the second approach; you can try the first one on your own:

After selecting the milestone, the page will be refreshed and the issue will now be added to the selected milestone. If you watch carefully, you can see a small icon and the name of the milestone next to it:

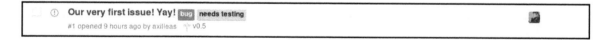

Using milestones to see which issues are resolved or are yet to be resolved

When dealing with hundreds of issues, bug reports, and enhancements, it is nice to have an overview of what is resolved and what is not.

Let's add another issue to the milestone and then immediately close it, as we learned in the *Creating an issue* section. In the context of the milestone, this will be considered as complete. Head over to the milestones page. You will see that the bar is now half full (at **50%**):

Tips and tricks

The README files are essential for your project as they add useful information to the start page. Let's briefly explore this feature and then learn about keyboard shortcuts.

Learning about the README file

The README file is used to provide information about your project. Its content is automatically shown on the front page of your repository, so it is always a good idea to provide one file.

GitHub checks whether the README file comes with an extension; if it is supported for rendering, it automatically gets formatted according to its implementation.

For example, a README file can have a .md extension that stands for markdown, a .rst extension that stands for restructured text, and a .adoc extension that stands for AsciiDoc.

If the extension is not supported, then GitHub treats it like a regular text file and no formatting is done.

For a list of supported markups, go to https://github.com/github/markup#markups.

Navigating easily with keyboard shortcuts

GitHub has the nice feature of supporting keyboard shortcuts. You can see which shortcuts are supported by hitting **?** on any page. A dialog box will pop up with all the supported shortcuts for that particular page. To see all the shortcuts, click on the **Show All** link.

Summary

In this chapter, you learned how to create your first repository and explored its main page. You also learned how to effectively use the issue tracker in order to track your project's bugs, feature requests, and so on. Moreover, you learned how to use labels and milestones to better group the issues.

In the next chapter, we will learn about wikis, as well as GitHub's feature concerning code release.

2
Using the Wiki and Managing Code Versioning

In the previous chapter, we explored the main page of a repository and we covered the basics of its issue tracker.

GitHub also provides a wiki-style place to add your project's documentation. You can create as many pages as you like and also grant public access to it so that everyone can edit it.

In addition, when you are the creator of a product and have users that rely on it, you will want it to be as stable as possible. Versioning helps to maintain an achievable goal. GitHub provides the right tools to release versions of your code, which in reality are just snapshots in time. Whenever you believe your project is ready to go out into the wild, whether bugs are fixed or new features are added, you can use the **releases** feature and deliver versioned tarballs to the world.

After finishing this chapter, you will have learned how to create, edit, and maintain a wiki by providing a home for your documentation that will complement your project.

You will also learn how to create a new release out of an existing branch or tag accompanied with optional release notes. This way, the end user can understand the changes from any previous versions.

This is what we will cover:

- Using the wiki:
    - Why wikis are a nice place to document your project
    - Creating a new wiki page
    - Deleting a page
    - Introduction to Markdown

- How to add a sidebar and a footer to your wiki
- Watching a wiki page's commit history and reverting to a previous state if needed
- Managing code versioning:
  - Creating a release
  - Editing a release
  - Pushing a tag from the command line
  - Marking as prerelease
  - Making a draft of a release
  - Uploading your own files
- Tips and tricks:
  - Subscribing to new releases via atom feed
  - Editing the wiki locally

Using the wiki

When you first create a new repository, a wiki attached to this project is also created. It is enabled by default and everyone can add new content or modify existing pages. If you want to change this behavior, you can refer to `Chapter 6`, *Exploring the User and Repository Settings*, which shows you how to accomplish this.

Why wikis are a nice place to document your project

Documentation is not to be taken lightly. To paraphrase a famous quote, with great projects comes great documentation.

Although there are many tools that convert markup files, such as Markdown to HTML, you may not want to use an external page to host your documentation. Enter GitHub wiki.

Creating a new wiki page

Select the **Wiki** tab (the one with the book icon) in order to head over to the wiki. Since our wiki has no content yet, the page doesn't exist. In this case, GitHub prompts you to create the first page. Go ahead and hit the green button.

Every time you add a new page to the wiki, the process is the same. At the top, there is the title. This is the only field that is mandatory in order to create a wiki page, as this is also used to form the URL from which you will have access to the page:

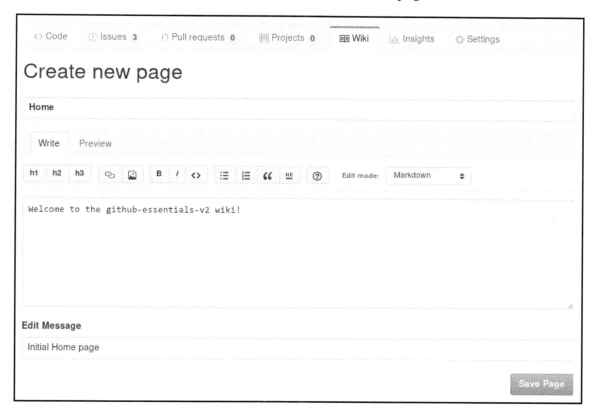

When the very first wiki page is created, GitHub uses the title Home by default. Even if you pick another name, the **Home** page is created automatically and is used as the front page of your wiki. The name Home behaves in the same way that README does for repositories, and it cannot be deleted.

Below the title area, there are two tabs. When the **Write** tab is active, you can begin to write in the blank area below. If you choose to write in a markup language, the **Preview** tab renders the text and shows you how it will be presented when you save the page.

Below the title, there is a nice toolbar that has the most common actions such as headers, bold text, italics, and lists. At the time of writing this book, GitHub supports nine markup languages to choose from. Pick one from the **Edit mode** drop-down list and the text will be rendered accordingly. For every language you pick from the menu, there is a little help page with the most common actions. Hit the question mark icon to see the help area.

Finally, when you are ready to save the page, you can provide a short message describing what the changes were about. Consider it like a Git commit message. Later, when we explore the page's history, the edit message will come in handy.

Whenever you are ready, press the **Save Page** button and the page will be created as follows:

Deleting a page

Every page except **Home** can be deleted. In order to do this, go to the page you want to delete and hit the **Edit** button at the right corner. As you will see later, deleting a page does not necessarily mean that it is purged forever. Read ahead and learn how to undo things.

A Markdown-powered wiki – an introduction to Markdown

While GitHub supports multiple markup languages, we will explore Markdown as it is the most well-known one.

Let's create another page, named `Installation`, with some content as follows:

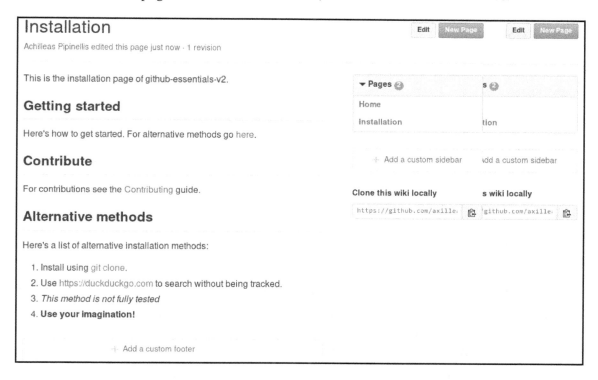

I have used several Markdown elements and hitting **Preview** will show you how the page will be rendered when it is saved. After you hit the **Save Page** button, the new **Installation** page will look like the following:

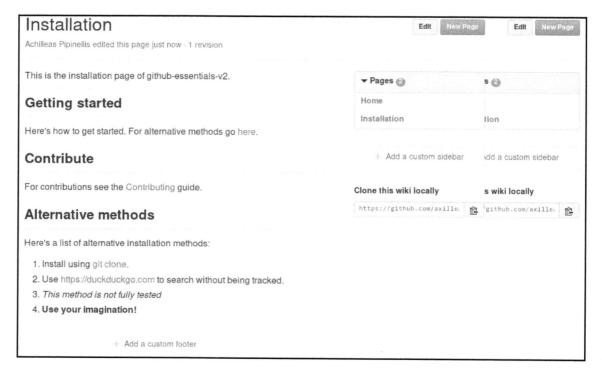

Some elements worth mentioning are the links. There are two kinds of links: external and internal. External ones are written by giving the full URL including the FQDN, whereas internal links only get called with the page name.

You can have external links that display the actual URL by surrounding them with <>, such as `<https://duckduckgo.com>`, and you can also include some random text such as `[git clone](https://git-scm.com/docs/git-clone)`. Inside the brackets, you can add any text you want, followed by the actual link inside parentheses. Be careful to not leave any spaces between the second bracket and the first parenthesis.

Internal links are useful when you want to link to another page of your wiki. Imagine you have 42 pages and you have to type the whole URL whenever you want to refer to another page. GitHub implements MediaWiki's markup in that case. Use double brackets (`[[]]`), and inside them, put the name of the wiki page you want to link to. In our example, I used `[[Contributing]]` and this will create a link to another page. Notice that if the link does not exist, it is rendered in red. If you click on it, you will be redirected to create the page.

When creating headers, you use # before the text. The number of # defines the header style that will be used. Each header gets a separate anchor link, which you can see if you place your mouse over it on a saved page. This anchor link can then be used to reference internal links.

In our example, you can see that I created three headers, namely `Getting started`, `Contribute`, and `Alternative methods`. In `Getting started`, I placed an interlink with a reference to `Alternative methods`. The piece of Markdown that did this is `[[here|Installation#alternative-methods]]`. This style introduces two new areas to explore.

Firstly, you can see that an alternate text can be used much like with external links. The only difference is that both the alternate text and the link are placed inside the double brackets separated by a pipe (`|`). Secondly, you can see how the call to the internal reference link is made. The page title goes first followed by the octothorp sign (#) and last is the header. It is important to understand that the header, as part of the interlink, gets transformed, whereas empty spaces are replaced with hyphens (–) and all special characters (`?`, `'!`, and so on) are lost.

You can always use the preview to test whether an anchor link will be rendered correctly.

Internal links are only supported inside the same wiki. You cannot link to another wiki with an internal link. In this case, you will have to use external links.

We have only scratched the surface regarding Markdown. You can read more about it in the nice cheat sheet at `https://github.com/adam-p/markdown-here/wiki/Markdown-Cheatsheet`.

How to add a sidebar and a footer to your wiki

If you have write access to a wiki, you should be able to see the **Add a custom sidebar** and **Add a custom footer** buttons.

GitHub has a default sidebar where it places all the pages of the wiki. This might not be useful since they are shown in name order and sometimes you want users to be able to access important information without searching too much.

Much like any other wiki page, the sidebar can be written in a markup language that GitHub supports. In the following example, I used `Markdown`:

As you can see, I used a bulleted list and placed links on each item. Indenting an item (one or more spaces) will provide the following result:

Like the sidebar, you can also create your own custom footer. For example, I used two external links with custom text, as you can see in the following screenshot:

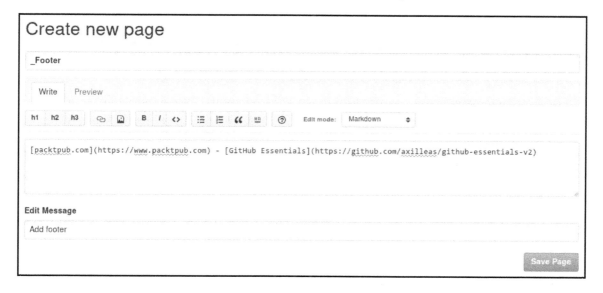

After all modifications, we get a nice wiki page with our custom sidebar and footer:

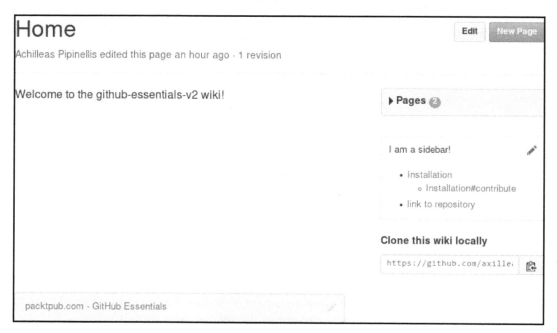

Watching a wiki page's commit history and reverting to a previous state if needed

Would you be surprised if you were told that a wiki is essentially a separate Git repository? In the *Tips and tricks* section, we will see how to clone a wiki locally, make changes, and push back to GitHub.

As with all Git repositories, there are commits and a history log. Each page gets a filtered log of the commits and changes it has undergone. One quick way to access the history log is to click on the revisions link on each page. This can be found under each page title. Take, for example, the **Home** page which has three revisions:

Home

Achilleas Pipinellis edited this page just now · 3 revisions

Another way to view a page's history is by using the **Page History** button which can be found when you edit a page.

One other way to see the history log is to append /_history to your page. So, for example, https://github.com/axilleas/github-essentials-v2/wiki/Home becomes https://github.com/axilleas/github-essentials-v2/wiki/Home/_history.

Here is what my **Home** page log looks like:

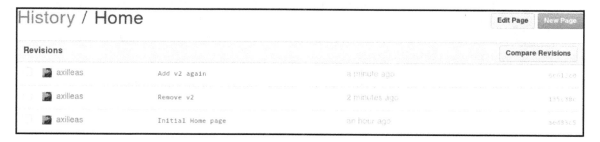

From the preceding screenshot, you can get a lot of useful information. You can see that the username of the person who made the change comes up first in the history table. In this example, there is only mine, but in a wiki with many collaborators, you can easily tell who made what change. Then, you get the commit message which is super useful because you can tell from a glimpse what the change was about. The third column is about the time the change was made and, finally, there is the commit SHA of the change.

Now, let's use the power of reverting when things go south. Firstly, create a new page, save it, and then delete it. We cannot go to that specific page's history log since it is no longer there, so we need to head over to the main **History** page, the mother of all pages. Since this page is hidden, you need to manually append /_history to your main wiki page.

In order to revert things, you need to use the **Compare Revisions** button. You can choose between one or two revisions to revert from:

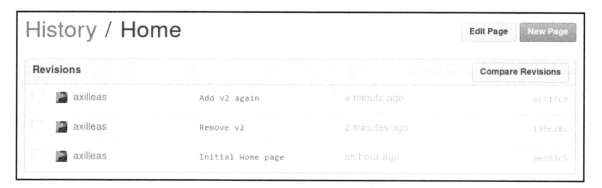

You can tell the default GitHub commit messages from the custom ones since they follow the pattern Created/Updated/Destroyed Title of page (language), where language is the markup language that was used to create the page.

Here, we chose two, but since they are one after another in the commit history, choosing only the last one would be the same. It's like comparing the changes between git show HEAD and git diff sha2 sha1, where sha2 is the last commit SHA and sha1 is the one before it. The diff is the same.

After hitting the `Compare Revisions` button, we will see the change that was introduced with this commit:

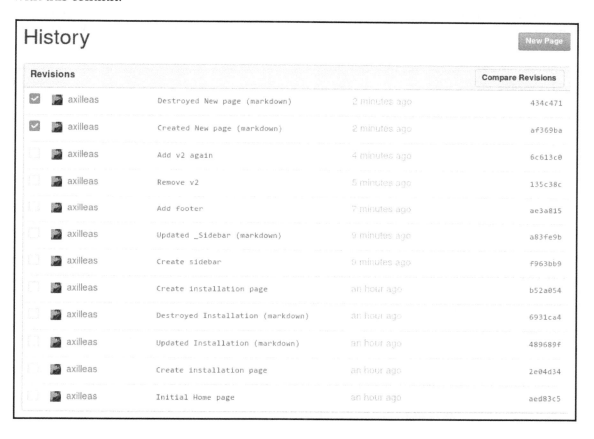

Let's bring back the deleted page by hitting the **Revert Changes** button. At the time of writing this book, every time I tried to revert the deletion of a page, I was presented with a 500 internal server error. Despite the error, go back to the **History** page, and you will see that the revert was indeed performed and the deleted page was brought back from the grave:

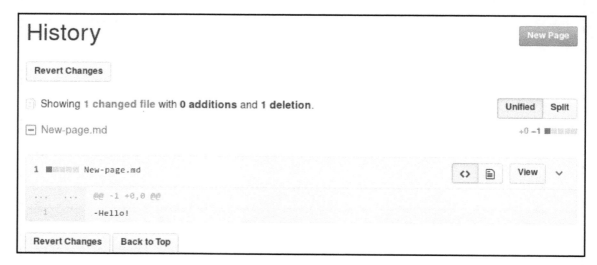

You can see that the commit message of the revert references the two commits that created and destroyed the page respectively.

 Sometimes, you will not be able to compare any two revisions and revert due to conflict. In this case, GitHub will warn you with a message: **This patch was not able to be reversed**.

That's all there is to know about GitHub wikis. Next we will focus on managing code releases with the tools GitHub provides.

Managing code versioning

In the world of software management, almost every piece of software is shipped with a version. It is a way to declare its evolution over time, usually with the addition of enhancements or bug fixes. GitHub leverages the power of Git and provides a simple interface to ship your versioned software.

Creating a release

In GitHub, the notion of a release is tightly tied to Git tags. You can see the existing tags, if any, from the same menu where you change a branch, as shown in the following screenshot:

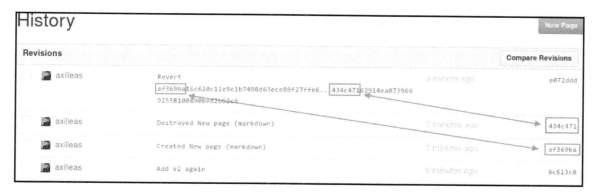

If you visit the **Releases** page and there is no tag created yet, you will be prompted to create one. Creating a release will automatically create a tag.

Let's click on the **Create a new release** button. The following page will appear:

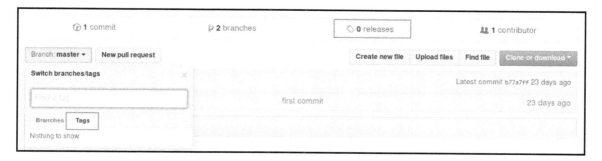

You only need to fill in the name of the **Tag version** box; everything else is optional. If the tag name you provide already exists, you will be presented with a duplicate tag name notification.

Your tag name can be any arbitrary value, but it is highly recommended to follow the semantic versioning scheme. To briefly describe what semantic versioning is: a release number consists of three numbers separated by dots in the form of MAJOR.MINOR.PATCH. You should then increment the following:

- The MAJOR version when you make incompatible API changes
- The MINOR version when you add functionality in a backwards-compatible manner
- The PATCH version when you make backwards-compatible bug fixes

You can read more at http://semver.org/.

One great way to name your tags is to match the existing milestones. From the previous chapter, we already had a v0.5 milestone so let's also name the new tag v0.5. Start typing it and if the tag does not exist, you will see the **Excellent! This tag will be created from the target when you publish this release** message.

You can choose the target branch or commit from the drop-down menu as shown in the following screenshot:

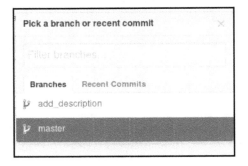

If you choose a branch, a tag pointing to the latest commit in that branch will be created. If you instead go to the **Recent Commits** tab, you can choose from a number of recent commits to create a tag from.

For the sake of our example, let's choose the master branch and enter a release title. Optionally, but recommended, you can add a description of what this release is about. I like to consider the description like writing a blog post of what changed in this release.

You can, of course, use Markdown like almost everywhere in GitHub and use the **Preview** button to see how it will be rendered:

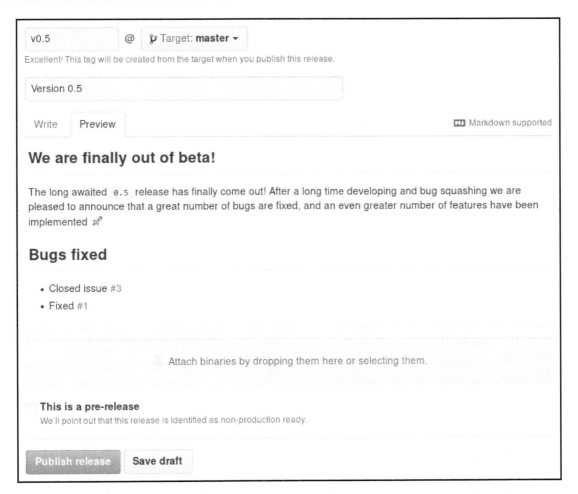

If you think everything is in order, hit the **Publish release** button. You can always edit any release anytime, so do not worry if you miss something. The following screenshot explains all the information about a release:

 If a release title is not provided, the tag name will be shown instead. Likewise, if a description is not provided, the latest commit message of the tag will be shown instead.

Editing a release

In order to edit a release, you can either click on the **Edit release** button next to the release under the **Releases** page or visit the particular release and click **Edit** there.

Pushing a tag from the command line

Now, let's see how GitHub behaves when a tag already exists. I made a few changes to a file and created a new tag from the command line. Finally, I pushed this tag to GitHub as follows:

```
git checkout master
echo "0.5.1" > version.txt
git add version.txt
git commit -m "Release 0.5.1"
git push origin master
```

If you now visit the tags page, you will see the new tag above the one we made before. In the releases page, click on **Draft a new release**. We will choose an existing tag, so in the **Tag version** field, type v0.5.1. GitHub found out that the tag already exists so it informed us that this is an existing tag:

Give it a title, a brief description, and then publish it. Since the v0.5.1 tag refers to the latest commit rather than the previous release, it now gets marked as **Latest release**.

Marking as pre-release

A nice little decorative feature is that you can mark a release as a prerelease, meaning you can inform the users that it's not ready for production but that they can still download and test it. Let's make a prerelease of the develop branch, which contains new commits that do not exist in master yet:

```
git checkout master
git checkout -b develop
echo "0.6rc1" > version.txt
git add version.txt
git commit -m "0.6 pre-release"
git push origin develop
```

Create a new release out of the `develop` branch and name it `v0.6rc1`. This time, mark it as a pre-release by ticking the relevant option:

After publishing it, here is what the releases page will look like:

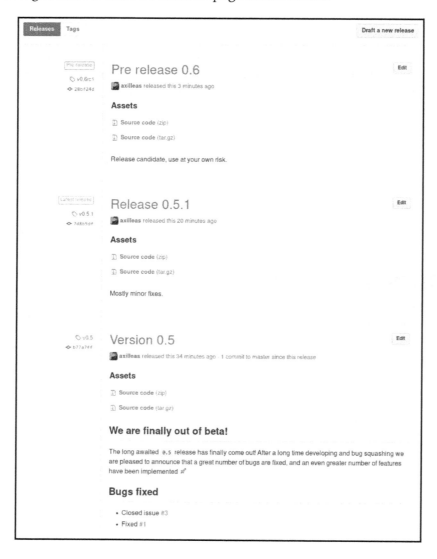

Making a draft of a release

If you tend to provide a detailed description with each release, you may find the draft feature quite useful. You can repeatedly edit a release while adding the required information and then save it as a draft. This way, you can spend less time on it when you need to publish it.

In order to make a draft of a release, do not click **Publish release**, but rather click the **Save draft** button. Back on the **Releases** page, you can see the draft release you just created:

You can edit it as many times as you want, and when the time comes to publish it, just click **Public release**. To delete a draft, click on the **Discard draft** button.

Since you are working on a draft, you don't have to worry about changing the tag of the release or any other information for that matter. Drafts can only be viewed by those who have write access to the repository, so it is not shown to the public until they are published.

Uploading your own files

There are cases where you might want to provide precompiled binaries for a variety of operating systems. For your Android application, it would be the apk files; for Windows, msi or exe; for Debian, deb; for RedHat, rpm, and so on.

When you create a release, there is a window at the very bottom that tells you to attach any binaries. Here, I uploaded a test `github-essentials.zip` file as you can see in the following screenshot:

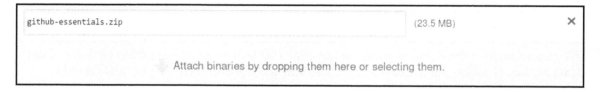

You can upload multiple files, but bear in mind that GitHub limits the upload size to 2 GB for each file. After you successfully upload the new binary and publish the release, you can see the files you manually attached along with the source code GitHub released for you:

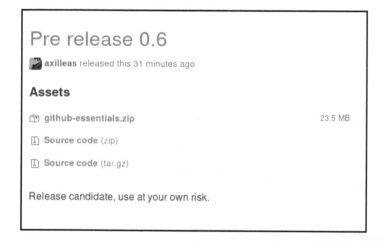

Tips and tricks

Here is a tip to get notified about new releases in an atom feed. Also, while you familiarize yourself with Git, you'll be happy to know that you can edit a project's wiki locally.

Subscribing to new releases via atom feed

If you are used to subscribing to feeds to learn the news regarding your favorite blogs, you will be happy to know that you can subscribe to get notified about new releases on GitHub.

Simply go to the releases page and append `.atom` to the end of the URL. For example, `https://github.com/diaspora/diaspora/releases` becomes `https://github.com/diaspora/diaspora/releases.atom`. Cool, isn't it?

Editing the wiki locally

As mentioned in the wiki commit history section, every wiki is a separate git repository. As such, you can clone it, make changes locally, and push back to GitHub.

It is powered by the `gollum` Ruby library that we will install and use to preview the wiki locally.

Installing gollum

The `gollum` library is packaged as a Ruby gem, and the easiest and quickest way to install it is to follow the official wiki entry at `https://github.com/gollum/gollum/wiki/Installation`. You can probably avoid installing it system-wide, but this is not within the scope of this guide.

Cloning the wiki and viewing the preview in your browser

Back on our wiki page, you should have noticed the download link. Every wiki repository has a remote URL encapsulated in green as shown in the following screenshot; essentially, it is the URL of the main Git repository with `.wiki` appended to the URL:

Use this URL and clone the wiki; then, run the `gollum` command inside that repository:

```
git clone https://github.com/axilleas/github-essentials-v2.wiki.git
cd github-essentials-v2.wiki
gollum
```

 Although not stated, you can also clone the wiki using the Git protocol and not HTTP.

If you see an output similar to the following, then `gollum` will successfully run and you can preview the wiki in your browser at `0.0.0.0:4567`:

```
[2015-07-26 01:09:34] INFO  WEBrick 1.3.1
[2015-07-26 01:09:34] INFO  ruby 2.1.6 (2015-04-13) [x86_64-linux]
== Sinatra (v1.4.6) has taken the stage on 4567 for development with backup
from WEBrick
[2015-07-26 01:09:34] INFO  WEBrick::HTTPServer#start: pid=20826 port=4567
```

The interface should be familiar with the GitHub wiki. Let's make a few changes.

Making changes locally and pushing to GitHub

Now that you have a running instance of the wiki, you can make changes in the browser much like in GitHub or use an editor such as `vim` or `emacs` and edit the files directly.

Since you already know how to edit the wiki in the browser, let's use an editor and change the `Installation.md` file. After the edit, save the file and commit it to Git. Take a second to see the log with `git log` and compare it with the history of the commits in GitHub (at `https://github.com/<username>/<repository>/wiki/_history`).

Now push the changes back to GitHub and visit the history page again. The new commit should be there along with the new change.

 If you want to write in a different markup language, other than Markdown, see the readme at `https://github.com/gollum/gollum#installation` for ways to install the necessary gems.

Summary

In this chapter, you learned the importance of documentation and how GitHub allows you to host a Markdown-powered wiki along with every project. Creating, deleting, editing, and reverting pages should by now be familiar terms.

What is the connection between releases and tags, you ask? Well, if you read the second part of this chapter, you should already know what connects them and how to create releases and distribute them to the public.

In the next chapter, you will see the management of organizations and teams. Read on and learn how to harness the power of collaboration.

3
Managing Organizations and Teams

In Chapter 2, *Using the Wiki and Managing Code Versioning*, we explored how you can accompany your project with documentation using the built-in wiki that GitHub provides, and we saw how to manage your code versions with GitHub releases.

It is important to know when to host a project under your namespace and when under an organization. With the organization, you have the ability to create teams and provide different access levels to people in the various repositories that are hosted under it.

In this chapter, we will go through creating an organization, inviting people, and granting them access to the repositories that are hosted under the organization. You will learn how to create teams and associate members of your organization to them as well as with the repositories.

We will cover the following:

- The difference between users and organizations
- Organization roles and repository permission levels
- Creating an organization
- Global member privileges
- Repositories
- Teams
- The People tab
- Organization settings

The difference between users and organizations

Apart from your user account that should be used only by yourself, GitHub provides the ability to create organizations managed by many users and, as we will see later, create teams within the organization.

GitHub is a collaborative place and as such, projects with high contribution traffic need a handful of people to help with the maintenance.

This might not be the only reason why one should create an organization, though. Leaving aside the practical reasons, an organization is usually created when there is more than one person, each having equal rights to the projects that the organization will host.

You can see, for example, big names such as Twitter, Google, or even GitHub itself that have organizations under which dozens of projects are hosted.

Organization roles and repository permission levels

GitHub allows you to choose among three roles for a person in an organization: owners, members, and billing managers. We will not deal with the latter; if you want more information on this, refer to `https://help.github.com/articles/adding-a-billing-manager-to-your-organization/`.

Owners have full access to the organization and are in the highest level of the permissions chain. As far as the organization is concerned, they can invite and remove people, create and remove teams, create and remove repositories, as well as manage the permission levels of all people and repositories. They can also edit the organization settings.

Being a member is usually the default role when a new person gets in the organization. The least a member can do is create a new team and add existing team members and repositories to it.

 The access level a member has over a repository can only be set by an owner.

A member can also be promoted to "Maintainer" for a particular team. With this access level, they can add and remove team members. Consider it like an extra hidden role on top of being a member. Anyone who creates a new team is granted the "Maintainer" role for that team.

Now, be careful not to mix organization permissions with repository permissions. There are four kinds of permissions that a repository can have: owner, admin, write, and read.

Owner is the top universal permission level that is granted to organization owners. With **Admin** access, one has owner privileges, but for the particular repository; you can push to it, delete it, add or remove a team, change the team's permission level, add outside collaborators, and so on. It is like creating a new repository under your personal namespace. With **Write** access, you can push to the repository; **Read** grants you read permission, which means clone and pull only.

For a comprehensive list of the various level permissions, check out GitHub's documentation at `https://help.github.com/articles/repository-permission-levels-for-an-organization/`.

Now that we have discussed the different access levels and permissions, let's create our first organization.

Creating an organization

In order to create an organization, find the cross button at the top header next to your avatar or visit `https://github.com/organizations/new` directly.

On the next screen, pick up an organization name and fill in a billing e-mail. For testing purposes, you can give your personal e-mail, which you can change later if you want. For open source projects, the creation of an organization is free, which is the default plan. If the organization will be owned by a business, you'll have to accept the corporate terms of service. All these options are summarized in the following screenshot:

As you type the name, GitHub searches behind the scenes if it is already taken, and if that is the case, a message appears saying that **Username is already taken**.

 As you will notice, there cannot be a user and an organization with the same name. Namespaces must be unique.

In the next step, you can optionally invite some people to be part of the organization. Search them by their username, full name or email, and then select them and click **Invite** to invite them to your organization. When done, hit **Finish**:

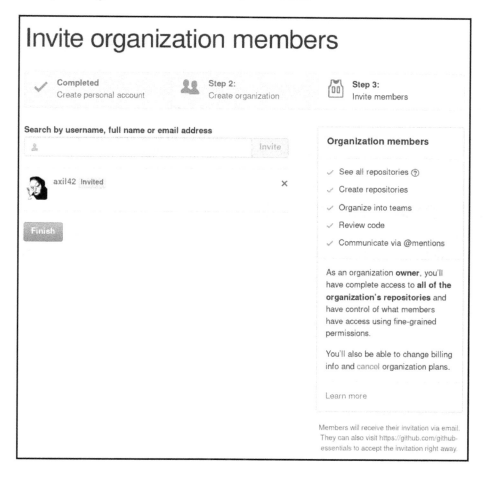

The first thing you will see after the creation is your organization's dashboard, as shown in the following screenshot:

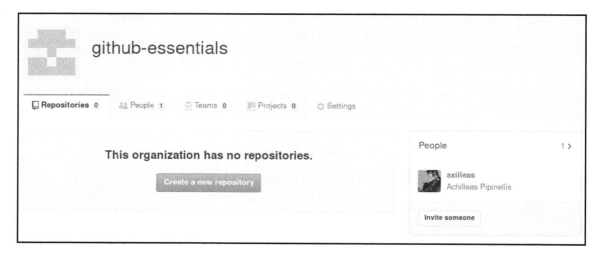

Before we dive into teams, people, and repositories, let's first check out some defaults by setting member privileges globally in the organization settings.

Global member privileges

Prior to inviting people and creating any repositories, let's examine two important settings and set some defaults. Head over to the **Settings** page and select the **Member privileges** tab:

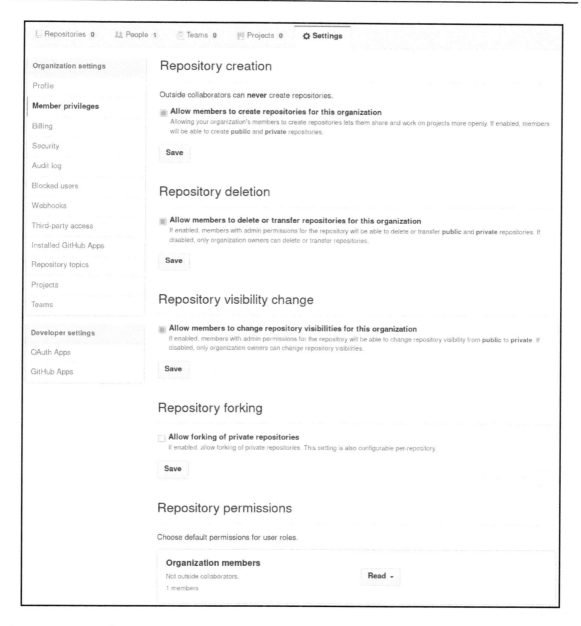

As you can see, there are various settings regarding the repositories. The first is about repository creation, and if enabled, any member of the organization will be able to create repositories under the organization namespace.

Enable this if you want to work more openly and disable it to be more strict. By disabling it, only owners will be able to create repositories. Outside collaborators (see the *Difference between Members and Outside collaborators* section) will not be able to create any repositories regardless of this option.

The next two options are for members with admin permissions on repositories. You can enable or disable the repository deletion and their visibility status to allow them to perform those actions on the repositories they have admin privileges on.

The next option is regarding the forking behavior of any private repository inside the organization. By default, it's disabled and members of the organization will not be able to fork private repositories.

The last option is regarding the default repository permissions that organization members have on all repositories, new or old. You can choose from four options: **Admin**, **Write**, **Read**, and **None**. The **None** option is the least privileged one and it means that members can only clone and pull public repositories. With **Read** access, a member can clone and pull every repository, public or private. **Write** access means that apart from read access, members can also push to the repositories. Lastly, **Admin** access will give every member the ability to pull and push to a repository as well as change its settings.

Throughout the rest of the chapter, the examples will be based on members being able to create repositories, and the default repository permission level will be **Read** unless otherwise noted.

We will explore the rest of the settings later in this chapter.

Repositories

So, the first tab on your new dashboard is **Repositories**, and since there is none at that time, GitHub urges you to create one.

Once you hit the **Create a new repository** button, you will be taken to a familiar page. If you read Chapter 1, *Brief Repository Overview and Usage of the Issue Tracker*, you will notice that the only thing that changes when creating a repository is the namespace. If I wanted, I could have created the repository under my username by choosing it from the drop-down menu.

After you fill in the information and the repository is created, you can upload the code from your computer and start working on it. You might have noticed in the repository's landing page when it was first created, that GitHub has a message to add teams and collaborators:

Give access to the people you work with

You should give access to the collaborators and teams you need to work with.

Add teams and collaborators

If you want to grant access to certain people immediately, then you should follow that route. For our purposes, given that this is a new organization, we must first learn about teams and their differences with outside collaborators as well as the different permissions on repositories.

Teams – a great way to grant selective access to your organization projects

A team is how you control different access levels in your repositories. Next, we will see how to create a team and add members to it.

Creating a team

As with most cases in GitHub, you can create a team in different ways. The apparent way is to head over to the **Teams** tab and create a new team by clicking the **New team** button:

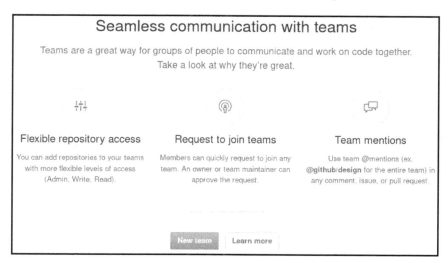

Another way to create a team is to head over to the **Settings** of an organization repository, and under the **Collaborators and teams** tab, hit the **Create new team** button. Notice that only a repository that lives under an organization namespace will have the **Teams** option. If you edit a personal project, you can only see the **Collaborators** box.

When you first create a new team, you will be presented with the following form:

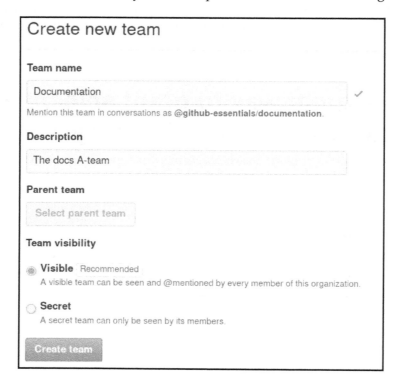

The team name is mandatory and the action is two-fold. You can enter a human-readable text with punctuation and capitalization, but notice that the name that will appear in the URL is converted to lowercase. For example, GitHub Core will be github-core. Any special character is stripped and converted to a dash (–).

You can put an optional description and then choose whether this team will be publicly visible or secret. A secret team will only be visible by its members and the owners.

Since GitHub supports nested teams, you are also presented with the option to choose the parent team that this team should be a child of. In case this is the very first team you create, there will be no parent, so this option will not be available.

After the team is created, you will be taken to the team's page where you can see who the team members are and what repositories this team has access to. You will be able to start a discussion with the members of that team and also edit the team's settings, such as change its name or even delete it:

Inviting people

The whole point of having teams is to have people in them. So far, you were the only member of the organization; let's invite someone to join the team.

 You can only invite people that are already registered GitHub users.

Head over to the **Teams** tab and select the team you want to invite someone to. Go to the **Members** tab and hit **Add a member**. Start typing the username and GitHub will sort out until it finds the right one:

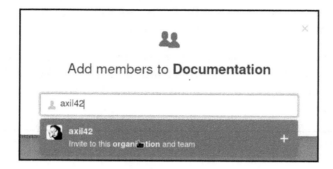

After you select the person, you can see that GitHub will tell you that there's one pending invitation. If you click on the **1 pending invitation** link, a modal will be revealed where you can edit the invitation:

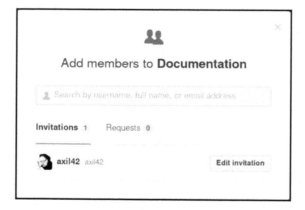

By default, the role one has when invited to a team is **Member**. If you want to change this to **Owner**, you can edit the invitation, change the role, and optionally assign different teams. You can cancel the invitation as well:

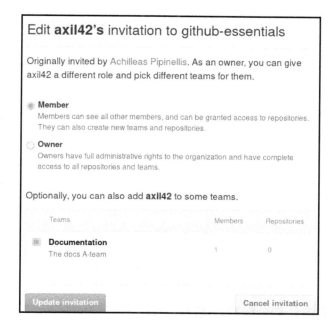

Edit **axil42's** invitation to github-essentials

Originally invited by Achilleas Pipinellis. As an owner, you can give axil42 a different role and pick different teams for them.

○ **Member**
Members can see all other members, and can be granted access to repositories. They can also create new teams and repositories.

○ **Owner**
Owners have full administrative rights to the organization and have complete access to all repositories and teams.

Optionally, you can also add **axil42** to some teams.

Teams	Members	Repositories
Documentation The docs A-team	1	0

Update invitation   Cancel invitation

 Only owners can invite new people to a team or the organization. A person has to be an organization member, for team maintainers to be able to add them to teams.

Accepting an invitation

GitHub will send out an email notifying the invited person about the invitation. In it, there is a link to follow that lands you to the organization page where you can accept the invitation or you can just ignore the email and visit the organization page directly.

Here I visited the organization's page as the person who got invited and as you can see I am presented with a message to join the organization:

axilleas invited you to join the **github-essentials** organization an hour ago.   **View invitation**

Either way, the final page where you will decide whether you will be joining the organization is as follows:

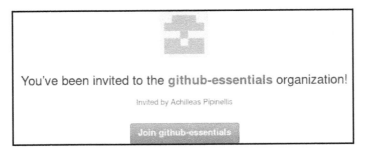

Let's accept the invitation and start working as part of the organization. After accepting, you will be able to see who the people are, the repositories, and the teams you have access to.

Team member permissions

As a maintainer of the team, when you visit the **Members** tab of your team's page, you can change a member's team access. Check the checkbox of one or more team members to change their membership. Once done, you'll notice that a dropdown appears. From there, you can either remove the selected members from the team or change their role. Let's click on the **Change role** link and change the role to **Maintainer**:

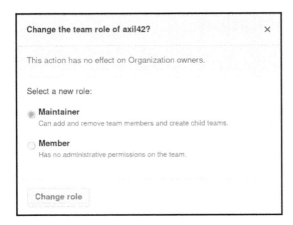

After you promote a member to maintainer, they will have more privileges, and the **Maintainer** label will be added next to their username:

axil42   Maintainer

A maintainer can now add or remove team members, edit the team's settings, and even delete it.

Requesting to join a team

There may be occasions where a member wants to get in another team that has more privileges on a repository. If you are already a member of an organization, you can ask a member to join an existing team. Let's break it down in steps and see how this is done.

Step one – as a user

Head over to the team you want access to, select the **Members** tab, and you will notice a **Request to join** button in the teams you are not a member of yet. Click on it and wait for your request to be reviewed by an administrator.

Once you request to join the team, an owner or a team maintainer will have to accept your request. If you now visit again the **Members** page of the team, you can see the **Cancel pending request** button. This way you know that your request has not yet been approved, and as you might have guessed, you can cancel it.

Step two – as an owner or team maintainer

By the time you request to join a team, an email notifies the owners and team maintainers about your request to join that team. As an owner or team maintainer, by visiting the **Members** tab of the team in question, you can see that there is a pending request:

Click on it and accept or reject the request:

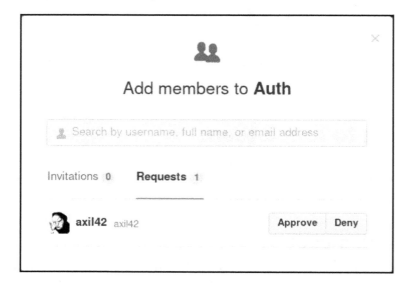

Adding repositories to a team

Assuming there's one or more repositories created under the organization, it's now time to add a repository to a team and explore the privileges of a team upon it. Remember that only owners can perform this action for all teams and team maintainers only for the team that they are maintainers of.

There are two ways to pair a team with a repository and vice versa. The first way is to search for a repository within a team and the second way is to search for a team within a repository.

Let's try the first one. Head over to the team that you want to add repositories to, and at the **Repositories** tab click the **Add repository** button and start typing the name of the repository to add:

As you can see, the default access to this repository is **Read**. This is the default access level that we have set in the *Global member privileges* section. Regardless of the global option, you can set different permissions on each repository that the team has access to:

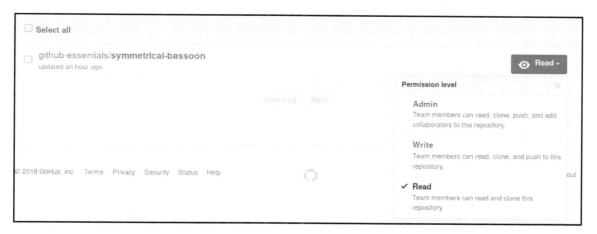

 Team members cannot change the repository access level, but can remove the repository from a team.

Now, if you head over to the repository's settings under the **Collaborators & teams** tab, you can see the team that is added:

Team discussions

Much like adding comments to an issue, members of a team can discuss things that may not be suitable to an issue itself. You can start a discussion under a team's landing page:

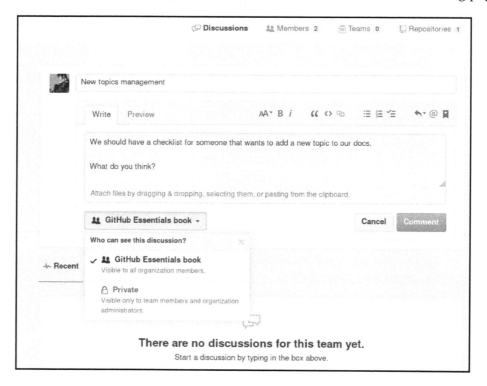

When starting a new discussion you can choose it to be visible to the whole organization or just to the team members.

The People tab

The **People** tab is where, as an owner, you can manage the organization members' privileges:

From the previous screenshot, you can see that, as an owner, you have a higher overview of the members in your organization. Let's examine what all of these settings mean.

The **2FA** mark simply means that a member has not enabled Two-factor authentication. From a security perspective, you would want every member of the organization to have enabled 2FA to prevent a potential account compromise that would lead to gaining access to the organization's repositories.

The next thing is the visibility of the organization membership. Each user must set the visibility for themselves. Set it to **Private** to hide your membership and choose **Public** to publicize it. If you publicize it, the organization's avatar will show in your profile.

Next, you can see how many teams each member is part of. Clicking on the number will show you the exact teams.

Lastly, there's the organization roles. Only owners have the ability to change a member's organization role and you can set it to either **Member** or **Owner** via the **Change role...** link:

The **Manage** button takes you to an individual's management page. Let's take a good look at it.

Managing access levels

Selecting **Manage access** will take you to a person's management page:

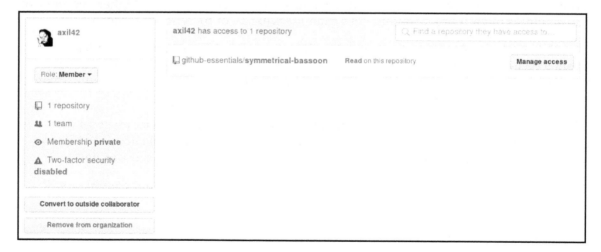

On the left-hand side box, you can see the same information as shown in the **People** dashboard. From here, you can change the member's role, even remove them from the organization, purging every permission they might have on the organization's repositories. The outside collaborator option will be covered in the next section.

On the right-hand side, you can see all the repositories they have access to and can manage their access level to every single one of them. Let's explore this setting by hitting the **Manage access** button:

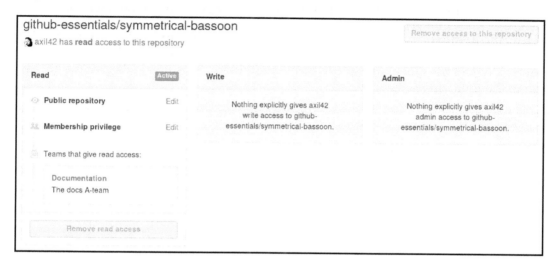

According to what you have set in the global settings access, as we saw in the *Global member privileges* section, you can see the access level in the particular repository. The access levels are also taken from the specific privileges a team has on a repository, as explored in the *Adding repositories to a team* section, which can override the global defaults.

Let's make a test and set the global setting to **Write** and see what happens. Click on the **Edit** button of the **Membership privilege** setting under the **Read** box. Then, change **Default repository permission** to **Write**, accepting GitHub's prompt, and go back to the previous page to see how it changed:

Even if the person was not a member of the team that would grant them write access, they would still have the **Write** access to the repository since this is now the global default. Also, notice how **Remove write access** is grayed out. Since the global default and the access that the team grants are the same (**Write**), there is no point of demoting a member's access level.

Similarly, the **Remove access to this repository** button on the top-right is grayed out. What this does is remove the access completely, which means in order to see this button enabled, you must have set the global repository access permission to **None**. Let's give it a go, as shown in the following screenshot:

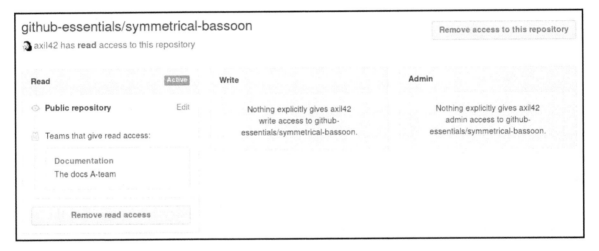

Removing the access to this repository is going to remove that person from the team that granted them access in the first place.

That's all there is to it when it comes to managing a member's access to a repository. Let's go ahead and finally see what these **Outside collaborators** are all about.

Difference between Members and Outside collaborators

As the name suggests, outside collaborators are non-organization members with repository access. Much like you can give write access to another user in your personal repository, you can give them write access to individual organizational repositories without being members.

At present, no one outside our organization has access to a repository. If you visit **Outside collaborators** under the **People** tab, GitHub will tell you that there are no collaborators yet:

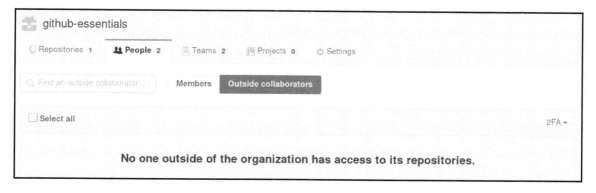

Let's add an outside collaborator by going to a repository's **Settings** in the **Collaborators & teams** tab:

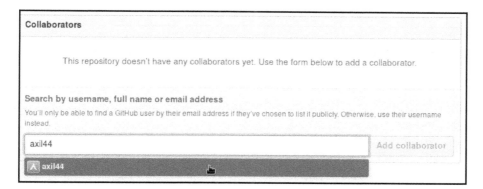

After selecting the user, hit the **Add collaborator** button:

Notice that the default access level is **Write** and not **Read**, which is set globally for the repositories. The default repository permission only applies to organization members, not to outside collaborators.

Once the user has accepted the invitation, you can head over to the organization's **People** page and select **Outside collaborators**. From this page, you can manage a collaborator's access and even invite them to the organization. Click on the wheel button and select **Manage** to manage their access:

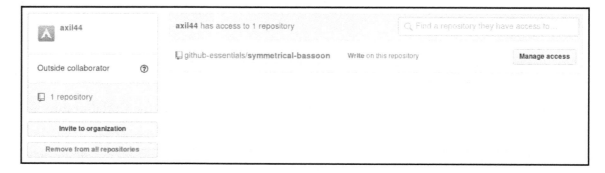

This particular user has **Write** access to one repository, and we can see that this is an outside collaborator. By going to **Manage access**, you can remove the user's write access to the repository or remove their access altogether:

Demoting to an outside collaborator

Just as you can be promoted to a member if invited, you can also be demoted. Under the **People** tab click on a user's username to manage their access:

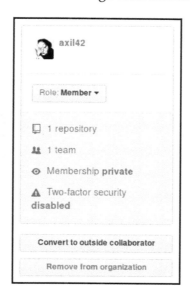

When converted to an outside collaborator, any repository access level that was given to this person in a team will be retained.

Organization settings

So far, we have only explored the **Member privileges** setting. Let's see the rest of them by heading over to the **Settings** page of an organization.

Profile

From the profile page, you can change the organization's name and its description, add a URL and a profile picture, rename the organization namespace, and even delete it:

After making all of these changes, you can see that the landing page of your organization will be a little bit prettier:

Security

Under the **Security** tab you can require all the member of the organization to enable two-factor authentication for maximizing security.

Audit log

If you have ever worked in a Unix environment, you should know that almost everything that is done in the system gets logged somewhere (usually under `/var/log/`). In the same way, GitHub logs most actions in what it calls an audit log.

While I was performing all the team creation, membership, and repositories examples, I got quite a big audit log:

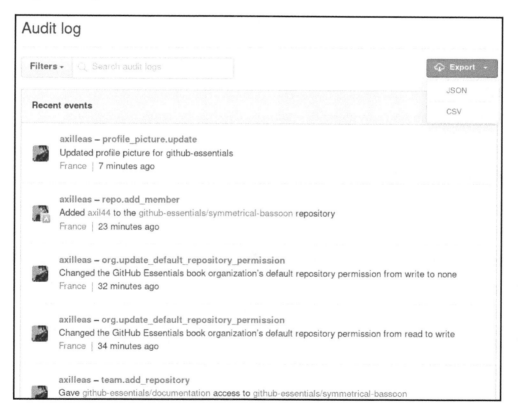

You can see what user made what action and the time this was performed. To better explore the log, GitHub provides the option to extract it in CSV or JSON format. You can even use the search function to filter specific events.

Third-party access

Third-party access is an advanced setting. Some applications and many web apps have a way to interact with GitHub and gather information about repositories, teams, user data, and so on. This is accomplished by the feature rich API that GitHub provides.

By default, this is set to be restricted. This means that if as a user you authorize an application, for example, to read all your repositories, it will not have access to the organization ones.

For more information, you can read GitHub's documentation at `https://help.github.com/articles/about-oauth-app-access-restrictions/`.

Teams

Under the **Teams** tab you can globally enable or disable the team discussions.

Tips and tricks

Here are some tips and tricks that complement what you have learned so far.

How to transfer a repository to an organization's namespace

There will be times where a repository of yours fits better under the umbrella of an organization. In this case, you can transfer it under the organization's namespace. You are able to transfer repositories to organizations only if you are at least their member.

Head over to your project's **Settings** and in the "Danger Zone" area you will see a **Transfer** button:

A modal will appear where you have to confirm by providing the repository's name and the organization that you wish this to be transferred to:

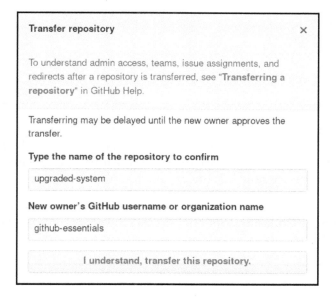

If you are a member of the organization, in the next step, you get to choose if you want any other teams to have access to this repository:

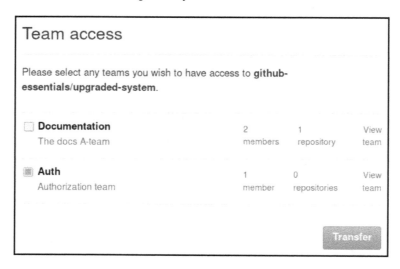

Once ready, hit **Transfer**. GitHub will notify you that the transfer might take a few minutes, but if the repository is relatively small with a few collaborators, it will take an instant. If you watch closely in your dashboard where your repository list appears, you will notice that your previous repository now has the organization's namespace before it.

If you head over to the repository's **Settings** in the **Collaborators & teams** tab, you will see that you are listed under **Collaborators**. In this case, the access is set to **Write** since this is the default global value:

 If you transfer your repository to an organization you are not an owner of, you might lose your admin privileges that you previously had on your repository. You can always ask an organization owner to grant you access.

How to convert a user account into an organization

For the reasons mentioned in *The Difference between users and organizations* section, one might want to turn a personal account into an organization. This can be easily done in the user's **Settings** under the **Organizations** tab.

You can then hit the **Turn username into an organization button**. Be sure that this is what you want because the action is irreversible.

In the next step, you have to choose an owner of the organization. Start typing and when the name appears, select it and hit **Choose**. Finally, hit **Create organization** to start the conversion process.

Mentioning teams

A cool way to get a team's attention in issues and pull requests is by mentioning the whole team. This is achieved with the following syntax: `@organization/team`. For example, to get everybody's attention in the **Documentation** team, you would use something like this: `@github-essentials/documentation`. Only the members and owners of the organization can mention teams.

Let's create an issue and see how this works. Head over to a repository that is under your organization and create a new issue and try to mention a team:

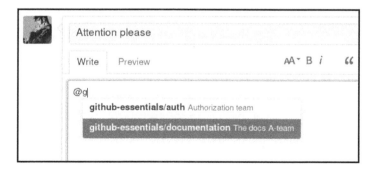

In case you are part of the team or are an owner, you will receive an email and a notification that will appear on your page at `https://github.com/notifications`:

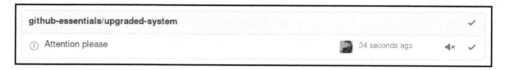

 The auto complete results are restricted to repository collaborators and any other participants on the thread, so it's not a full global search.

Organization feed only in dashboard

When you are on the landing page of `https://github.com`, you can see your dashboard activity of your repositories and the people you follow. Sometimes, when you are a member of many organizations the information might be cluttered, so you would rather filter the activity to one organization.

Just choose the organization you wish to filter from the drop-down menu and you will see activities only from that organization. If you want, you can also subscribe to the news feed using the atom feed link found at the bottom:

Summary

That's it! Congratulations on finishing this chapter. You should now be familiar with almost all organization features. Creating teams, inviting people, and managing repository access should feel much more easier.

If you found it difficult to follow, I would recommend you to just play with it, make a test organization, and go through the chapter again. Full disclosure, this is how this chapter was written. I created an organization, a second test user, and through trial and error this chapter was born. Given that GitHub has released new organization features in beta, I had to do a lot of testing. I think the result was worth the effort.

In the next chapter, we will explore GitHub's strongest point: collaboration and pull requests.

Collaboration Using the GitHub Workflow

4

In Chapter 3, *Managing Organizations and Teams*, we explored how you can create and manage organizations and teams that will further help you in collaborating with others.

GitHub is a great tool for collaboration and, as such, it has come up with a workflow based on the features it provides and the power of Git. It has named it the GitHub workflow (https://guides.github.com/introduction/flow).

In this chapter, we will learn how to work with branches and pull requests, which are the most powerful features of GitHub. Here's what we will cover:

- Learning about pull requests
- Peer review and inline comments
- Merging the pull request
- Tips and tricks

Learning about pull requests

Pull request is the number one feature in GitHub that made it what it is today. It was introduced in early 2008 and has been used extensively among projects since then.

While everything else can be pretty much disabled in a project's settings (such as issues and the wiki), pull requests are always enabled.

Why pull requests are a powerful asset to work with

Whether you are working on a personal project where you are the sole contributor, or on a big open source project with contributors from all over the globe, working with pull requests will certainly make your life easier.

Think of pull requests like chunks of commits, and the GitHub UI helps you clearly visualize what is about to be merged in the default branch or the branch of your choice. Pull requests are reviewable with an enhanced different view. You can easily revert them with a simple button on GitHub and they can be tested before merging, provided a CI service is enabled in the repository.

 CI stands for **continuous integration**. For more details, you can refer to the applications that GitHub integrates at `https://github.com/marketplace/category/continuous-integration`.

The connection between branches and pull requests

There is a special connection between branches and pull requests. In this connection, GitHub will automatically show you a button to create a new pull request if you push a new branch in your repository. As we will explore in the following sections, this is tightly coupled to the GitHub workflow, and GitHub uses some special words to describe the *from* and *to* branches. As per GitHub's documentation:

> *The base branch is where you think changes should be applied, the head branch is what you would like to be applied.*

So, in GitHub terms, head is your branch, and base is the branch you would like to merge into.

Creating branches directly in a project – the shared repository model

The shared repository model, as GitHub aptly calls it, is when you push new branches directly to the source repository. From there, you can create a new pull request by comparing between branches, as we will see in the following sections.

Of course, in order to be able to push to a repository, you either have to be the owner or a collaborator; in other words, you must have write access.

Creating branches in your fork – the fork and pull model

Forked repositories are related to their parent in a way that GitHub uses in order to compare their branches. The fork and pull model is usually used in projects when you do not have write access, but are willing to contribute.

After forking a repository, you push a branch to your fork and then create a pull request in the parent repository, asking its maintainer to merge the changes. This is common practice for contributing to open source projects hosted on GitHub. You will not have access to their repository, but, being open source, you can fork the public repository and work on your own copy.

How to create and submit a pull request

There are quite a few ways to initiate the creation of a pull request, as we will see in the following sections.

The most common one is to push a branch to your repository and let GitHub's UI guide you. Let's explore this option first.

Using the Compare & pull request button

Whenever a new branch is pushed to a repository, GitHub shows a quick button to create a pull request. In reality, you are taken to the compare page, as we will explore in the next section, but some values are already filled out for you.

Let's create, for example, a new branch named `add-gitignore` where we will add a `.gitignore` file with the following content:

```
git checkout -b add-gitignore
echo 'password' > .gitignore
git add .gitignore
git commit -m 'Add .gitignore'
git push origin add-gitignore
```

Next, head over to your repository's main page and you will notice the **Compare & pull request** button:

From here on, if you hit this button, you will be taken to the compare page. Note that I am pushing to my repository following the shared repository model, so this is how GitHub greets me:

What would happen if I used the fork and pull repository model? For this purpose, I created another user to fork my repository and followed the same instructions to add a new branch named `add-gitignore-2` with the same changes. From here on, when you push the branch to your fork, the **Compare & pull request** button appears whether you are on your fork's page or on the parent repository.

This is how it looks if you visit your fork:

The following screenshot will appear if you visit the parent repository:

In the last case, you can see from which user this branch came from (**axil42:add-gitignore-2**).

In either case, when using the fork and pull model, hitting the **Compare & pull request** button will take you to the compare page with slightly different options:

Since you are comparing across forks, there are more details. In particular, you can see the base fork and branch as well as the head fork and branch that you are the owner of.

GitHub considers the default branch set in your repository to be the one you want to merge into (base) when the **Create pull request** button appears.

Before submitting it, let's explore the other two options that you can use to create a pull request. You can jump to the *Submitting a pull request* section if you like.

Using the compare function directly

As mentioned in the previous section, the **Compare & pull request** button takes you to the compare page with some predefined values. The button appears right after you push a new branch and is there only for a few moments. In this section, we will see how to use the compare function directly in order to create a pull request.

You can access the compare function by clicking on the **New pull request** button next to the branch drop-down list on a repository's main page:

This is pretty powerful as you can compare across forks or, in the same repository, pretty much everything—branches, tags, single commits, and time ranges.

The default page when you land on the compare page is as follows; you start by comparing your default branch with GitHub, proposing a list of recently created branches to choose from and compare:

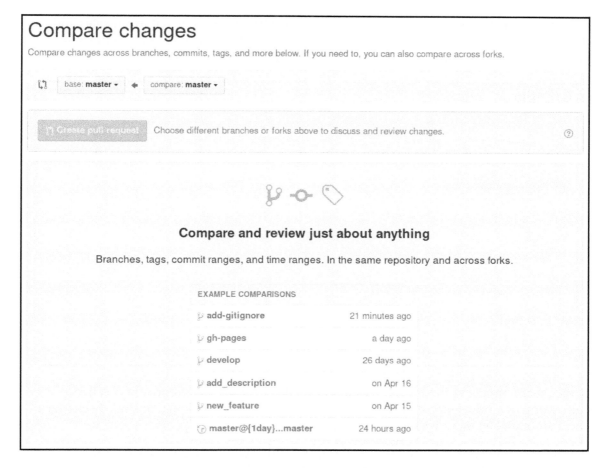

 In order to have something to compare to, the commits of the base branch must be older than what you are comparing to.

From here, if I choose the `add-gitignore` branch, GitHub compares it to a master and shows the differences along with the message that it is able to be merged into the base branch without any conflicts. Finally, you can create the pull request:

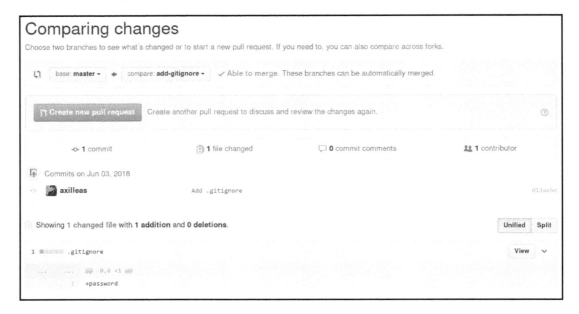

Notice that I am using the compare function while I'm at my own repository. When comparing in a repository that is a fork of another, the compare function slightly changes and automatically includes more options, as we have seen in the previous section.

As you may have noticed, the **New pull request** quick button is just a shortcut for using the compare function manually. If you want to have more fine-grained control on the repositories and the branches compared, use the compare feature directly.

Using the GitHub web editor

So far, we have seen the two most well-known method for initiating a pull request. There is a third way as well: using the web editor that GitHub provides in its entirety. This can prove useful for people who are not too familiar with Git and the Terminal, and can also be used by more advanced Git users who want to propose a quick change.

As always, according to the model you are using (shared repository or fork and pull), the process is a little different. Let's first explore the shared repository model flow using the web editor, which means editing files in a repository that you own.

The shared repository model

Firstly, make sure that you are on the branch that you wish to branch off; then, head over to a file that you wish to change and press the edit button with the pencil icon:

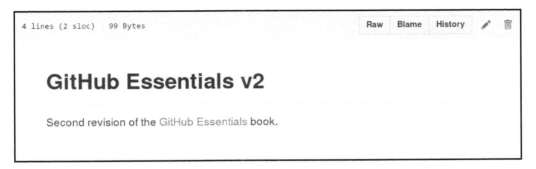

Make the change you want to that file, add a proper commit message, and choose **Create a new branch**, giving the name of the branch you wish to create. By default, the branch name is `username-patch-i`, where `username` is your username and `i` is an increasing integer starting from 1. Consecutive edits on files will create branches such as `username-patch-1`, `username-patch-2`, and so on. In our example, I decided to give the branch a name of my own:

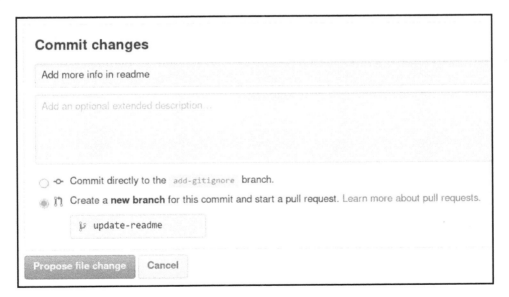

When ready, press the **Propose file change** button. From this moment on, the branch is created with the file edits you made. Even if you close the next page, your changes will not be lost. Let's skip the pull request submission for the time being and see how the fork and pull model works.

The fork and pull model

In the fork and pull model, you fork a repository and submit a pull request from the changes you make in your fork. In the case of using the web editor, there is a caveat. In order to get GitHub to automatically recognize that you wish to perform a pull request in the parent repository, you have to start the web editor from the parent repository and not your fork. In the following screenshot, you can see what happens in this case:

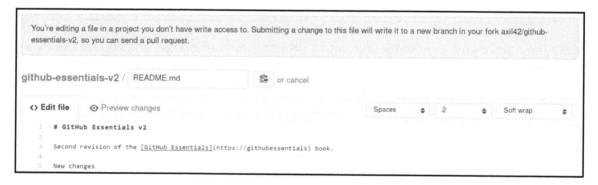

GitHub informs you that a new branch will be created in your repository (fork) with the new changes in order to submit a pull request. Hitting the **Propose file change** button will take you to the form to submit the pull request:

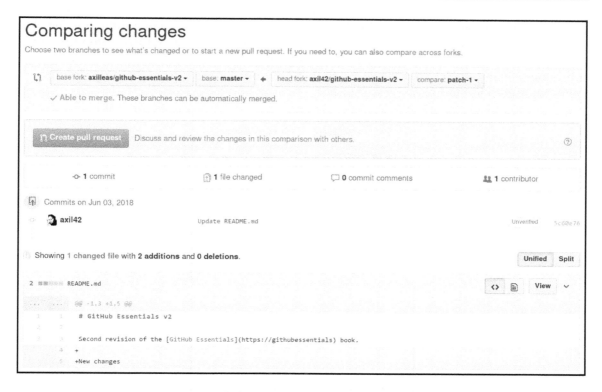

Contrary to the shared repository model, you can now see the base/head repositories and branches that are compared. Also, notice that the default name for the new branch is patch-i, where i is an increasing integer number. In our case, this was the first branch created that way, so it was named patch-1.

If you would like to have the ability to name the branch the way you like, you should follow the shared repository model instructions, as explained in the preceding section. Following that route, edit the file in your fork where you have write access, add your own branch name, hit the **Propose file change** button for the branch to be created, and then abort when asked to create the pull request. You can then use the **New pull request** quick button or use the compare function directly to propose a pull request to the parent repository.

One last thing to consider when using the web editor is the limitation of editing one file at a time. If you wish to include more changes in the same branch that GitHub created for you when you first edited a file, you must first change to that branch and then make any subsequent changes. How to change the branch? Simply choose it from the drop-down menu, as shown in the following screenshot:

Submitting a pull request

So far, we have explored the various ways to initiate a pull request. In this section, we will finally submit it.

The pull request form is identical to the form when creating a new issue. For more details, refer to Chapter 1, *Brief Repository Overview and Usage of the Issue Tracker*, the *Learning how to use the powerful benefits of the issue tracker* section.

If you have write access to the repository that you are making the pull request to, then you are able to set labels, milestones, and assignees.

The title of the pull request is automatically filled by the last commit message that the branch has or, if there are multiple commits, it will just fill in the branch name. In either case, you can change it as you see fit. In the following screenshot, you can see that the title is taken from the branch name after GitHub has stripped the special characters. In a sense, the title gets humanized:

You can add an optional description and images if you want. Whenever ready, hit the **Create pull request** button. In the following sections, we will explore how the peer review works and eventually merge the pull request.

Peer review and inline comments

The cool thing about pull requests is that you have a nice and clear view of what is about to get merged. You can see only the changes that matter, and the best part is that you can fire up a discussion concerning those changes.

In the previous section, we submitted the pull request so that it can be reviewed and eventually get merged. Suppose that we are collaborating with a team and they chime in to discuss the changes. Let's first check the layout of a pull request.

The layout of a pull request

Every pull request pretty much looks as follows:

From the previous screenshot, you can tell what the specific number of the pull request is. It is like an identifier within the repository and it is not separated from the issues count. Issues and pull requests share the same ID counter. So, in the preceding example, you can see that although this is our first pull request, it is numbered **#6**; the previous five were issues:

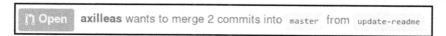

Then, there is the information that the pull request is **Open** and who wants to merge how many commits into which branch from which other branch:

Right below the information we just described, there are four tabs: **Conversation**, **Commits**, **Checks**, and **Files changed**. In **Conversation**, except for the comments that we will see in the following screenshots, GitHub also adds information about the events concerning the particular pull request. You can see the action and the time it occurred. For example, take a look at the following screenshot; even little changes such as adding a label are being recorded:

The **Conversation** tab is also where the final call takes place. This is where the button to merge the pull request resides, and you can see its status. The button is green, which means there are no conflicts between the changed files and the ones that are in the repository:

Finally, there is the comment form that is the same as in the issue tracker that we explored in `Chapter 1`, *Brief Repository Overview and Usage of the Issue Tracker*. You can leave any comments concerning the pull request here.

The **Commits** tab shows the commits made in this branch and the commits that are not yet in the branch you are merging into. For example, the `update-readme` branch has two commits that do not exist in `master`. GitHub shows the commits in chronological order along with other information, such as who the author is, and links to the commits:

The **Checks** tab is reserved for external services that talk to GitHub's API and can perform checks on the pull request. That can be a continuous integration service that tests the code, or one that checks if the pull request conforms to some guidelines. We won't get into any details since this is a very broad area outside the scope of this book, but you're free to read more on GitHub's documentation at `https://help.github.com/articles/about-status-checks/#checks`.

Finally, the **Files changed** tab shows the files that are changed in this pull request. There are two ways to see the differences in the commits. The default one is to see the changes in a unified way, with additions and deletions on the same page, as shown in the following screenshot:

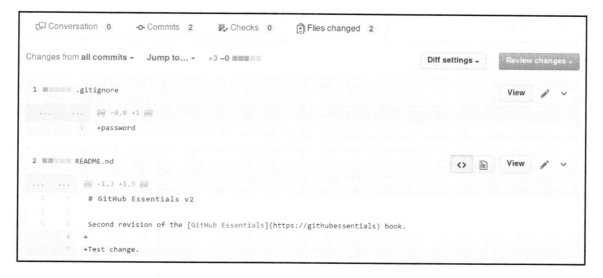

 Note that for each addition, GitHub marks a line with a green background color. On the contrary, if you were to remove some lines, they would show in pink. I will leave that to you as an exercise.

The other way is to choose **Split**, and GitHub will show the differences in a side-by-side view. Under the **Diff settings** drop-down menu, there's the option to see the changes in **Split** mode. Choose it and hit **Apply and reload** for the changes to take effect:

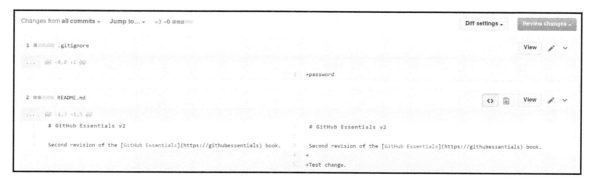

In the next section, we will further explore the **Files changed** tab since this is where the review process takes place.

The review process

To make the review process a bit easier to follow, there are a couple of features that are useful when dealing with a lot of commits and changed files.

The **Changes from** drop-down menu is helpful if you want to see the changes introduced by a single commit or a range of commits:

Next to it, the **Jump to** dropdown provides a list of all changed files that you can choose and jump to:

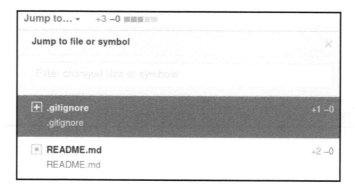

This might seem redundant when there's only two files, but it's powerful if there's a dozen of them as you don't have to manually scroll down the page and find what you're looking for.

In addition, this menu will become sticky as you scroll down a long page of changes so that you don't have to scroll all the way back up:

```
Changes from all commits ▾    Jump to... ▾   +23 −16 ■■■■        Diff settings ▾    Review changes ▾
      # essential
     -# Until https://github.com/gjtorikian/nanoc-conref-fs/issues/5 is fixed, can't update to v4.2
     -gem 'nanoc', ['>= 4.1', '< 4.2']
     +gem 'nanoc', '~> 4.7'
      gem 'nanoc-conref-fs', '~> 0.5'

      # rendering
     -gem 'nanoc-html-pipeline', '0.3.3'
     +gem 'nanoc-html-pipeline', '~> 0.3'
      gem 'gemoji', '2.1.0'
      gem 'html-pipeline-rouge_filter', '~> 1.0'
      gem 'extended-markdown-filter', '~> 0.4'
```

GitHub supports inline comments, so you can leave a comment under every changed line, as seen in the **Files changed** tab. When hovering over a line, you will notice the cross image, as shown in the following screenshot; click on it and the comment form will appear:

When writing a comment, you can either submit it right away as a single comment or start a review. When starting a review, the comment is submitted, but it doesn't notify the repository members. That way, you can submit comments in batches and notify the submitter of the pull request in one go. In the following example, there are two comments on the proposed changed files:

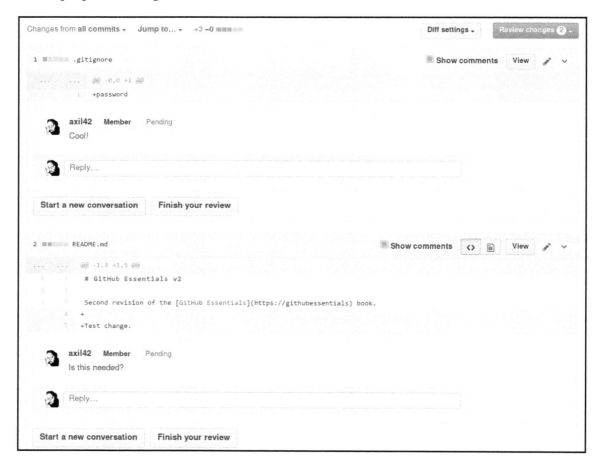

Notice that they are in pending status and they wait to be finally submitted for review. Once you're ready to finish your review, hit the **Finish your review** button under your comments or use the **Review changes** drop-down menu.

From there on, you have three options. The first one is just to **Comment** and ask nothing else from the submitter. The second option is to **Approve** the changes while leaving your feedback. Finally, the last one is to **Request changes**, usually in the lines where you commented on. Optionally, leave a review summary and click **Submit review**.

With a few comments on the diff and a request for changes, we can see a couple of things. First of all, inline comments count towards the overall conversation, so the **Conversation** tab should pick that number. Furthermore, since changes were requested, that is shown in the pull request widget at the bottom:

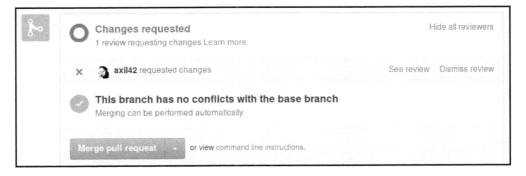

As the submitter of the pull request, you can click on the **See review** link and be taken to the review comments or hit **Dismiss review** if you think you have addressed all the comments. In the latter case, you will need to add a comment justifying your action.

Correcting mistakes

So far, we have seen how conversations begin, but what happens when the changes you made need some tweaking to be considered as ready to merge?

In this case, you can push new commits to the branch associated with the pull request and GitHub will pick up those changes and amend it. The new changes will show up and further feedback can be given. In *The review process* section, my evil twin, user `axil42`, raised a concern about a wrong line being committed. We will now make a new commit and push it to the `update-readme` branch and see what happens:

```
git checkout update-readme
sed -i 's/Test change/For more info, check the wiki/' README.md # replace
text
git add README.md
git commit -m 'Correct line in README.md'
git push origin update-readme
```

Back in GitHub, three changes occurred. Firstly, there was another commit added to the **Commits** tab. Then, in the **Files changed** tab, since the line on which the comments were relying on was removed, the comments no longer appeared. Instead, you can see that in the **Conversation** tab, this particular discussion was marked as outdated:

README.md	⚖ Show outdated

If you were by, any chance, in the **Files changed** tab while the last commit was pushed, GitHub would inform you about the changes and would urge you to refresh the page:

Merging the pull request

After the conversation took place, changes were made, and the peer review worked as expected, so it's now time to finally merge the pull request.

If you don't have access to merge the pull request, you should see the following result:

On the other hand, owners or collaborators with write access can also merge pull requests. In this case, you should see the **Merge pull request** green button. From the arrow next to it, you can optionally choose the merge method before merging it. There are three options, with the default one being the creation of a merge commit. Pick the one you want and hit merge:

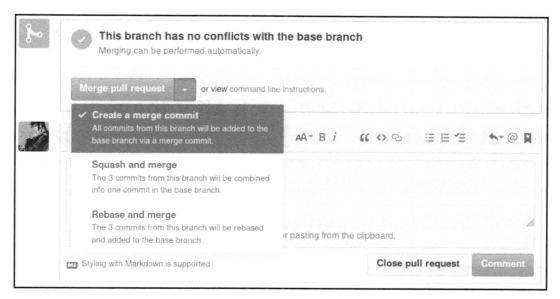

Pressing this button will not merge it immediately, but you will have another chance to confirm:

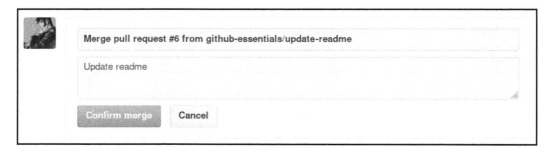

The commit message of this merge is the one in bold, and the one below that can be edited is the extended commit message, which, by default, grabs the pull request title. In the extended commit message, you can reference issue numbers with a special meaning. Read more in the *Tips and tricks* section of this chapter to learn how to automatically close issues from pull requests.

Once merged, you can see the green icons turning to purple. This indicates a merged pull request.

Removing/restoring a branch after the pull request is merged

In order to have everything cleaned up and tidy, GitHub offers removing the merged branch with a simple button right after the pull request is merged:

After the deletion is completed, GitHub makes this an action event. If you changed your mind, you can always restore the removed branch again using the **Restore branch** button, as shown in the following screenshot:

Reverting a pull request

There are cases where you might want to revert a pull request, and GitHub makes this extremely easy. Right after the merge happens, there will be a **Revert** button next to the merge action:

Pressing this button will create a new pull request with opposite commits to the ones the previous pull request included.

Tips and tricks

So far, we have explored most of the functionality of pull requests. Let's see a couple of things that leverage their power even more.

Closing issues via commit messages

In Chapter 1, *Brief Repository Overview and Usage of the Issue Tracker*, in the *Tips and tricks* section, you learned how to reference issues inside the issue tracker. Extending this ability, you can reference issue numbers in commit messages in order to close some issues when the commit is merged to the default branch.

For this action to be triggered, you have to use some keywords. For example, Closes #42 in the commit message will close issue 42 when that commit is merged with the default branch.

As per the GitHub documentation, the following keywords will close an issue via a commit message:

- close
- closes
- closed
- fix
- fixes

- fixed
- resolve
- resolves
- resolved

Let's take, for example, an open issue such as the following one and note down its number, which in this case is **2**:

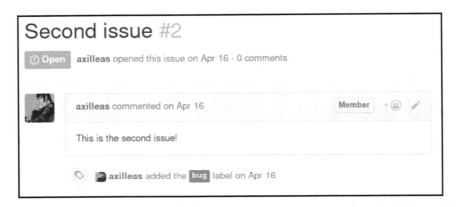

Then, make a commit, which, in its message, has one of the preceding keywords, referencing the preceding issue number. We will follow the GitHub flow that we learned in this chapter, so first create a new branch:

```
git checkout master
git checkout -b fix-issue-2
```

For the sake of our example, I modified one file in the repository and then committed it with the following:

```
git commit -m 'Demo example of closing issues. Closes #2'
git push origin fix-issue-2
```

Then, open a new pull request to merge the branch we just created, and merge it like you learned in this chapter.

Going back to the issue tracker, you will no longer see issue #2 among the open issues. Instead, go to the closed ones and you will see that issue #2 is closed. GitHub provides all the necessary information:

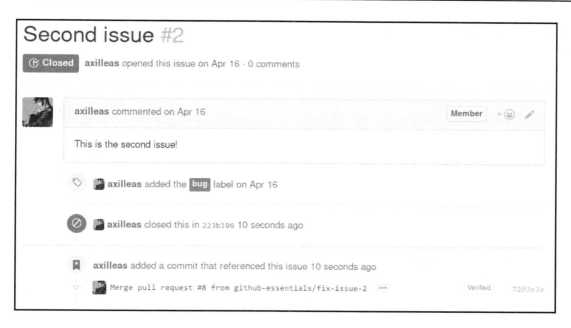

For more information on closing issues via commit messages, check out GitHub's documentation at `https://help.github.com/articles/closing-issues-using-keywords/`
.

Task lists in pull requests

A nice feature when submitting a pull request, which is a work in progress, is the task lists. A work in progress pull request would mean that you work on a specific feature/bug, and so on, but there are many changes that cannot be committed in one go and you also need someone to peer review your progress while working on it.

In this case, you will find task lists quite handy. Let's create a pull request and, in the description box, add the following:

```
- [ ] First item
- [ ] Second item
- [ ] Third item
  - [ ] Fourth nested item
  - [ ] Fifth nested item
- [x] Sixth item , closes #2 (marked as resolved)
```

The result will be a list with checkboxes where you can manually check/uncheck the items whenever you complete a task:

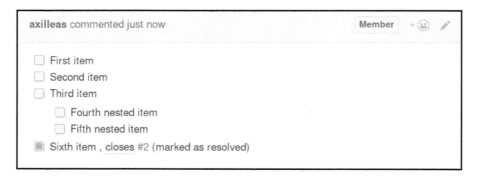

If you head over to the pull request tracker for an overview, you will see the task list showing the following pull request:

This works for cross references as well, and since we referenced issue 2 in the task list, this will be recorded in the issue:

 Task lists can also exist in issues.

Downloading the diff of pull requests

For the hardcore fans of patch and diff files, GitHub has this nice feature where you can view and download the changes that a pull request introduces in the format of a patch. Simply append `.patch` to the URL of a pull request. For example, `https://github.com/github-essentials/github-essentials-v2/pull/6` becomes `https://github.com/github-essentials/github-essentials-v2/pull/6.patch`. The content of this file includes all the commits of a pull request.

A global list of your open pull requests

Right next to the search bar at the top, there is a link named **Pull requests** that takes you to a page where you can find all your pull requests that are open. Go to `https://github.com/pulls` directly to visit this page.

Adding a LICENSE file using the web editor

Much like you can edit the already existing files, you can also create new ones. In this case, we want to add a license file, and GitHub provides a way of choosing among a variety of them. On your repository's initial page, under the **Code** tab, click the **Create new file** button:

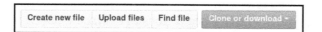

On the next page, type `LICENSE` so that the **Choose a license template** button appears:

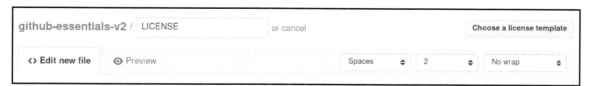

Click on it and choose a license from the ones GitHub provides. Once done, hit **Review and submit**:

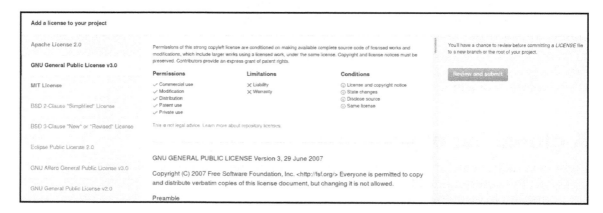

In the next step, you are called to commit your changes straight to the default branch or create a pull request. Once the changes are merged, if you navigate to the repository's main page, you will see a link to the license file that you just committed:

Here is an easter egg. You can type LICENCE the British way or type LICENSE the American way. GitHub is smart enough to respect this language quirk and, in fact, it doesn't even care about the case of the letters. For what it's worth, typing LiCENce or liCEnSe is still considered the same! Lastly, the word copying is also considered to be a synonym to license, so the previous examples apply to this word as well.

Creating new directories using the web editor

Apart from creating new files, you can also create new directories via the web editor. Just click on the **Create new file** button, like we demonstrated in the previous trick of choosing a license, and type the name of the directory ending with a slash (/). You can repeat this process as many times as you like.

The only caveat is that empty directories are not being picked up by Git and, by extension, by GitHub, so you will have to provide a file at the end if you want to commit this change.

Summary

In this chapter, we explored the GitHub workflow and the various ways to perform a pull request, as well as the many features that GitHub provides to make that workflow even smoother. This is how the majority of open source projects work when there are dozens of contributors involved.

In the next chapter, we will see how to make pretty, static web pages that are hosted solely on GitHub and how to read the analytics that GitHub provides for each project.

5
GitHub Pages and Web Analytics

In this chapter, you will learn how to build web pages around your project, hosted for free and exclusively on GitHub, by using Jekyll, which is a static site generator, or by providing your own HTML pages.

Continuing our exploration of GitHub features, next comes the ability to visualize a repository's data. GitHub has implemented some nice features, such as graphs that can depict, among other things, the commit activity of the contributors and the traffic a repository gains, as well as the commit history in a network graph.

We will cover the following:

- GitHub Pages
- Web analytics
- Tips and tricks

Let's dive in!

GitHub Pages

At the end of 2008, GitHub announced GitHub Pages (`https://github.com/blog/272-github-pages`), a static-site hosting service. Static sites have seen a significant increase over recent years, and GitHub played a big part in that. A static site is a site that contains pages written in HTML, CSS, and JavaScript. No server code, such as PHP, Ruby, or Python, is included, nor is a database required.

In order to create a functional website hosted on GitHub Pages, you must follow some conventions. Let's look in detail at how to create any of these pages.

Creating a user or an organization page

For users and organizations, a repository named `username.github.io` must be created, where `username` is your username or organization name, and files must be pushed to the `master` branch.

Create a new empty repository named after your username. After creating it, clone it locally and add a test `index.html` page (replace `username` with yours):

```
git clone git@github.com:username/username.github.io.git
cd username.github.io
echo 'Welcome to my first page!' > index.html
git add index.html
git commit -m 'Add the first webpage'
git push -u origin master
```

Right after the upload finishes, visit `https://username.github.io` (where `username` is your own username) and look at the results.

That's it! You can start writing your own HTML pages and push to GitHub. The changes are almost instant.

Creating a project page

Project pages are somewhat different to user/org pages; the source files of your website can reside in one of the three following locations: the `gh-pages` branch, the `master` branch, or a `docs` directory of the `master` branch. You can choose which one you want to use by selecting it under your repository's **Settings** under GitHub Pages.

For project pages, if there is a branch named `gh-pages` in the repository, then its HTML content is automatically served by GitHub. The project page will ultimately be accessible via `https://<username>.github.io/<repositoryname>`.

Here, I will create a `gh-pages` branch in the `github-essentials` repository, make a new `index.html` file, and commit and push to the `gh-pages` branch:

```
git checkout -b gh-pages
echo 'Welcome to my first project page!' > index.html
git add index.html
git commit -m 'Add index.html page'
git push origin gh-pages
```

Once `index.html` is uploaded, it will immediately be rendered under your page's URL. Since I uploaded it under my username (`axilleas`) in a repository named `github-essentials`, I know that the URL will be `http://axilleas.github.io/github-essentials`.

While you could manually modify the content of the project's website, GitHub provides a better automatic method to update the content of your web page in one go. Read the following sections to learn how to achieve this.

Choosing a theme to style your page

About four years after the launch of GitHub Pages, GitHub announced the addition of another feature, the GitHub page generator.

This is an easy way to bootstrap a website for your project with just a few clicks. Under each repository's settings, there is a section for **GitHub Pages** with the option **Choose a theme**:

When you select **Choose a theme**, GitHub helps you to create a single HTML page based on your `README.md` file with a variety of beautiful layouts to choose from, in an interactive step-by-step guide. This will work only on a `README.md` file that is present in one of the `gh-pages` or `master` branches. If the `README.md` file doesn't exist, GitHub will create one for you when you choose a theme for the first time.

> The formatting of the website's content is written in Markdown, which we have explored in `Chapter 2`, *Using the Wiki and Managing Code Versioning*. You can use its markup language to define headings and lists, add links, and so on.

When you are inside the theme chooser, you will be able to choose from the existing layouts. Each layout follows a pattern, and there are links and buttons that point to your repository's URL and the ZIP or TAR file downloads. When ready, hit **Select theme**, and the website will change its layout in a few seconds:

From now on, each time you change the README.md file, the changes will be automatically published in your website.

 Each time you choose a theme, a _config.yml file is committed to your repository with information about what theme is currently in use.

If you head over to the **commits** page, you can see that GitHub has some useful information about the build of your website. Clicking on the green check-mark icon will take you to the website:

Now that your website is up and running, let's look at how you can use your own custom domain.

Using a custom domain

Instead of using the classic GitHub Pages URL, you can use a custom domain name linked to your user/org GitHub page. This means you can tell GitHub that when someone asks for www.mydomain.rocks, it will serve the content that's published under username.github.io.

First, create a CNAME record in your DNS provider that will point www.mydomain.rocks to username.github.io. Then, head over to your repository's username.github.io **Settings** > **GitHub Pages**, add your domain name under **Custom domain**, and hit **Save**. From now on, every time you visit username.github.io, you will be redirected to www.mydomain.rocks. Similarly, a project page under username.github.io/repository-name will be redirected to www.mydomain.rocks/repository-name. Note that your custom domain will be served automatically by HTTPS. If the **Enforce HTTPS** option is not set, make sure you set it:

Using the www subdomain as your custom domain has some benefits over using just mydomain.com or another subdomain, such as blog.mydomain.com. Notably, that way, you automatically use GitHub's CDN and you are protected from DoS attacks. For more information about the kinds of domains you can use, visit GitHub's documentation at https://help.github.com/articles/about-supported-custom-domains/.

Let's now explore how you can leverage the power of a static-site generator to create more content for your website.

Introducing Jekyll

So far, we have learned how to create web pages manually by pushing HTML files or using the GitHub theme generator for project pages. However, there is another, more sophisticated way to build your website.

Every day, more and more people turn to using static websites for their personal projects, and even companies use it for their main sites or blog platforms. A static site is faster and more secure than one built with a server-side language, such as PHP. On the other hand, maintaining a static site and updating its content completely manually is a tedious task.

For these reasons, so-called static-site generators exist: applications that use templates, markup languages, and configuration files, and convert these to pure HTML pages.

GitHub Pages uses Jekyll, which is a static-site generator written in Ruby, and is among the top open source static-site generators (https://www.staticgen.com/).

In order to use Jekyll, you will need access to a terminal.

Installing Jekyll

In order to install Jekyll, refer to its documentation at https://jekyllrb.com/docs/installation/. If you encounter any problems, be sure to visit their troubleshooting guide at https://jekyllrb.com/docs/troubleshooting/#installation-problems.

Following installation, you can check whether it was installed correctly by running `jekyll` in your terminal. You should see an output similar to the following:

```
jekyll 3.8.2 -- Jekyll is a blog-aware, static site generator in Ruby

Usage:

  jekyll <subcommand> [options]

Options:
        -s, --source [DIR]  Source directory (defaults to ./)
        -d, --destination [DIR]  Destination directory (defaults to
./_site)
            --safe          Safe mode (defaults to false)
        -p, --plugins PLUGINS_DIR1[,PLUGINS_DIR2[,...]]  Plugins directory
(defaults to ./_plugins)
            --layouts DIR   Layouts directory (defaults to ./_layouts)
            --profile       Generate a Liquid rendering profile
        -h, --help          Show this message
        -v, --version       Print the name and version
        -t, --trace         Show the full backtrace when an error occurs

Subcommands:
  docs
  import
  build, b                Build your site
  clean                   Clean the site (removes site output and metadata
file) without building.
  doctor, hyde            Search site and print specific deprecation warnings
  help                    Show the help message, optionally for a given
subcommand.
  new                     Creates a new Jekyll site scaffold in PATH
  new-theme               Creates a new Jekyll theme scaffold
  serve, server, s        Serve your site locally
```

Customizing your page using Jekyll

Now we will create a new boilerplate site that `Jekyll` provides in order to start building on it. This is achieved with the `jekyll new path/to/site` command:

```
jekyll new website
```

Navigate to the new directory that was created and list the files:

```
cd website
ls -la
```

You should see the following directories and files:

```
.gitignore
404.html
Gemfile
Gemfile.lock
_config.yml
_posts/
about.md
index.md
```

Now, let's build the site locally and see how that looks:

```
jekyll serve --watch
```

Open your browser to `http://127.0.0.1:4000` and you should see the default Jekyll boilerplate site:

The –watch switch enables the autogeneration of files so that you don't have to stop and start the server all the time. However, if you edit _config.yml, you must restart the server by stopping and running the jekyll serve command again.

From there on, you can start hacking on the new website. For starters, try to edit _config.yml and change some options. After changing the title, description, and email, stop and start Jekyll again to see the changes in effect.

When you're happy with the changes, it's time to push to your GitHub repository's master branch for user/org pages, or to gh-pages if it's a project page. For a brand new project, you'd need to initiate a new Git repository inside the website directory; or, for an existing project, you'd need to move all those files Jekyll generated under the existing repository.

In the following example, I will assume a new user page is created from scratch. First, you'd need to create a new empty username.github.io repository on GitHub. Next, in the website directory, issue the following commands:

```
git init
git add .
git commit -m 'Init commit using Jekyll'
git remote add origin git@github.com:username/username.github.io.git
git push origin master
```

After a few seconds, GitHub should build the site, and you can visit your user page at username.github.io to confirm that all went well.

For project pages, make sure that baseurl in _config.yml reads /repository-name/, otherwise the CSS files won't be picked up correctly.

Read more about Jekyll

As you may have noticed, we have only set up the base for developing with Jekyll. For extensive documentation, refer to the Jekyll website at https://jekyllrb.com/docs/home/. You can find a list of sites that run Jekyll at https://github.com/jekyll/jekyll/wiki/sites.

Other helpful articles are, of course, the GitHub help pages about Jekyll:

- `https://help.github.com/articles/using-jekyll-with-pages/`
- `https://help.github.com/articles/using-jekyll-plugins-with-github-pages/`

Web analytics

Due to GitHub's nature, a repository contains a great deal of metadata, such as commits over time, who contributed what, the number of contributors, the number of forks, and even site referrals to various files.

GitHub provides some useful graphs and data, from which you can deduct the information you require under the **Insights** tab of a repository. Let's explore what's underneath.

Pulse

Pulse is an overview of a repository's activity. The default is to show the last week, but you can change the period from the drop-down menu on the right, by choosing 24 hours, 3 days, 1 week, or 1 month.

From here, you have a high-level overview of the merged and open pull requests, and open and closed issues, as well as the top committers for that period:

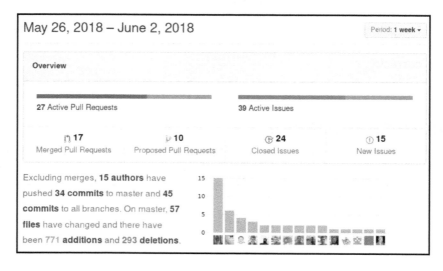

Contributors – additions/deletions

An overview of the top 100 contributors of a project can be seen at the **Contributors** tab. The graph is created by the data of the default branch of a repository and it depicts the commits from the beginning of the project until the current day:

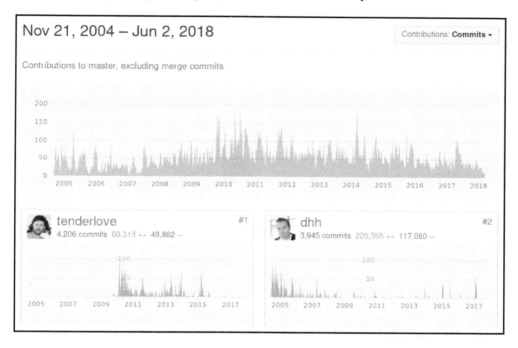

The default filter is the commit count. If you want to change to see who made the most additions or deletions, you can toggle the filter with the **Filter contributions** drop-down menu on the right:

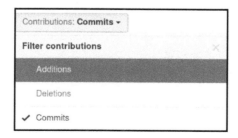

The data can be fine-tuned further by choosing a specific period from the graph by selecting an area. For example, to see the contributions data between 2015 and 2016, you would do the following:

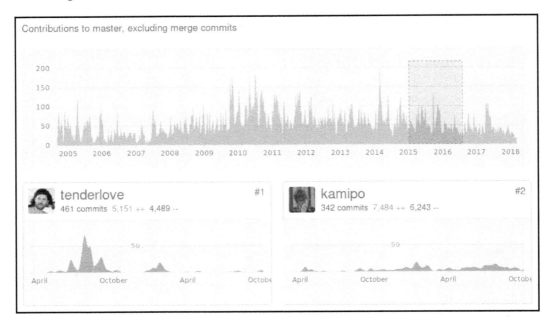

Community profile

In the **Community** tab, there's a checklist for the most important things you should have present in your repository so that it is friendly to outside contributors. You can see from the following screenshot that a README file, a contributing guide (`https://help.github.com/articles/setting-guidelines-for-repository-contributors/`), and a license (`https://help.github.com/articles/adding-a-license-to-a-repository/`) are already present, whereas a code of conduct file (`https://help.github.com/articles/adding-a-code-of-conduct-to-your-project/`) is missing.

In that case, GitHub will help you add one:

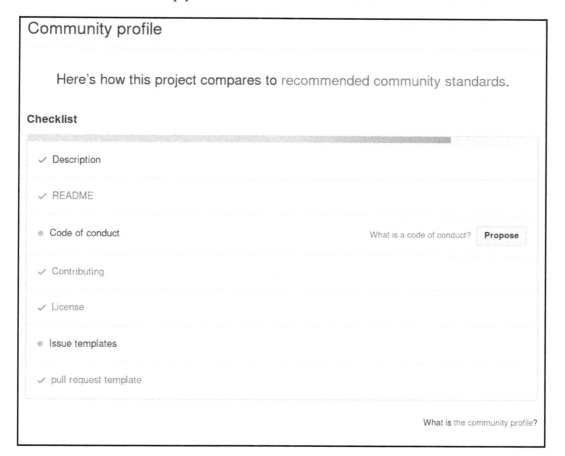

Commits over time

The **Commits** tab shows the commit activity during the previous year. In the upper bar graph, you can visualize the number of commits per week; if you click on one bar, the graph that appears below will show the number of commits per day of that particular week:

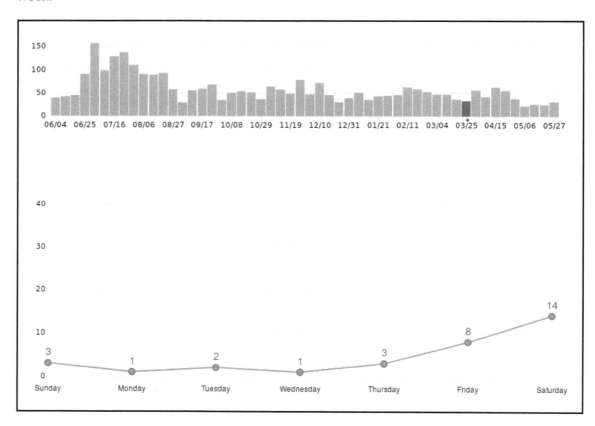

Code frequency

The **Code frequency** tab shows the weekly code additions and deletions:

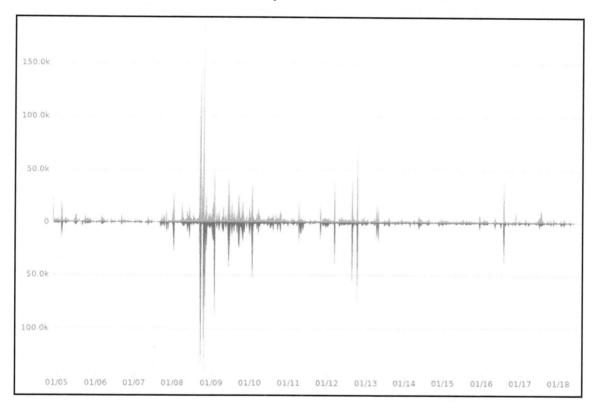

Dependency graph

Under the **Dependency graph** tab, you can see the dependencies and the dependent libraries of your project. At the time of writing, GitHub only supports Ruby and JavaScript, and checks whether your repository contains a Gemfile and package.json file, respectively. Once it finds one, it scans and lists all the dependencies, as well the dependencies of their dependencies:

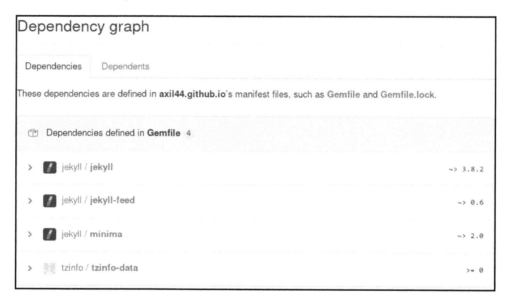

Apart from the dependency listing, GitHub also notifies you when a vulnerability is found in one of the libraries you use. For more information about the security alerts, read https://help.github.com/articles/about-security-alerts-for-vulnerable-dependencies/.

Network

The **Network** graph shows the branch history of the main repository as well as its forks. You can click and drag the graph or use your keyboard arrows to see the older history. To view how another fork deviates from its parent, click on the owner name and you will be transferred to that repository network graph.

Finally, you can click on the little bullets, and you will be transferred to that particular commit:

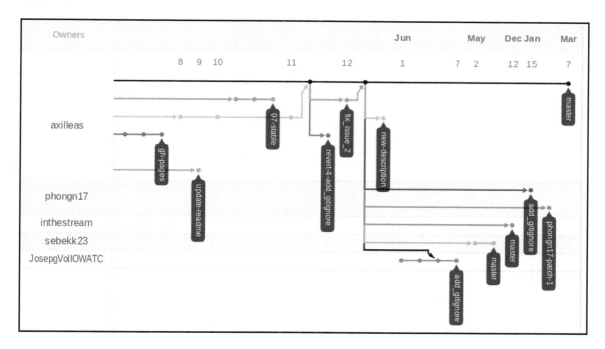

 If a project has many forks, GitHub will not be able to render the **Network** graph.

Forks

The **Forks** tab, as the name suggests, shows a list of forks of your repository:

Traffic

The **Traffic** tab is the only tab that can only be seen by project owners or team members. The higher the traffic a repository has, the more data is to explore. Generally, there information is available for a period of about two weeks.

In the first graph, you can see how many times a repository has been cloned in that period. By hovering the mouse on the bullets, you can clearly see the clones and unique cloners as GitHub names them, per day:

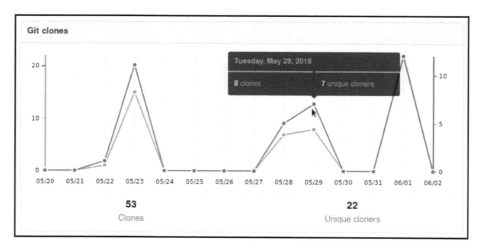

Likewise, you can see the total views for the last two weeks, as well as how many unique visitors your repository has had:

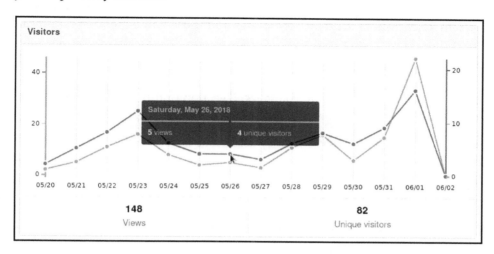

Right below these graphs are the referring sites and the popular content. Clicking on a site will take you to another page where the actual link appears. Search engines and GitHub's own search are excluded:

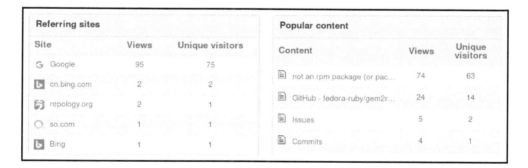

Tips and tricks

The next tip is to use some advanced techniques that use the GitHub API.

Making use of Github Pages' metadata with Jekyll

GitHub provides some metadata when using Jekyll for GitHub Pages. This means that you can add certain keywords in the Jekyll templates and these will be rendered automatically.

For example, you could add the `{{ site.github.project_title }}` variable, and the project title would be filled by GitHub automatically.

Following the example in the *Introduction to Jekyll* section of this chapter, we will add a new post to the Jekyll site.

Firstly, head over to the repository directory and make sure you are in the `master` branch and up to date:

```
git checkout master
git pull origin master
```

Next, copy the default post to have it as a reference (the dates in your site will differ):

```
cp _posts/2018-06-02-welcome-to-jekyll.markdown _posts/2018-06-02-testing-github-metadata-with-jekyll.markdown
```

Then, open the new file and remove all content except for the following:

```
---
layout: post
title:  "Welcome to Jekyll!"
date:   2018-06-02 11:42:46 +0200
categories: jekyll update
---
```

Edit it to look as follows:

```
---
layout: post
title:  "Testing GitHub metadata with Jekyll"
date:   2018-06-02 00:00:00
categories: jekyll github
---

The name of this project is {{ site.github.project_title }} and owned by
{{site.github.owner_name}}.
```

Commit your changes and push them:

```
git add .
git commit -m "Add new post"
git push origin master
```

After a few seconds, the post will appear on the front page and its content will have the variables rendered:

You can read more at https://help.github.com/articles/repository-metadata-on-github-pages/.

Summary

In this chapter, we learned the purpose of GitHub Pages and the various ways to upload your content. A quick introduction to Jekyll will hopefully provide a basis for further reading and use of this cool static-site generator.

We also ran through the various visualizations that GitHub provides, with the graphs and other tools that are part of every repository.

In Chapter 6, *Exploring the User and Repository Settings*, we will explore the user and repository settings.

6
Exploring the User and Repository Settings

In this chapter, we will explore the most important settings for both a user and a repository. There are many things you can do to personalize your experience in GitHub and many settings you can change in order to follow a specific workflow with your fellow teammates.

As a user, there is a lot of information you can set up on your user settings page, such as associating more than one email with your account, adding multiple SSH keys, and setting up two-factor authentication.

Similarly, some functionalities of a repository can be set up via its settings page. For example, you can enable or disable the wiki pages, or completely disable the issue tracker.

In this chapter we will cover the following:

- User settings
- Repository settings
- Tips and tricks

User settings

You can visit your user's settings page by navigating through the web interface (under your avatar's drop-down list) or by visiting `https://github.com/settings/profile` directly:

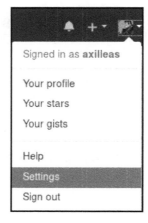

For example, here is what my settings landing page looks like:

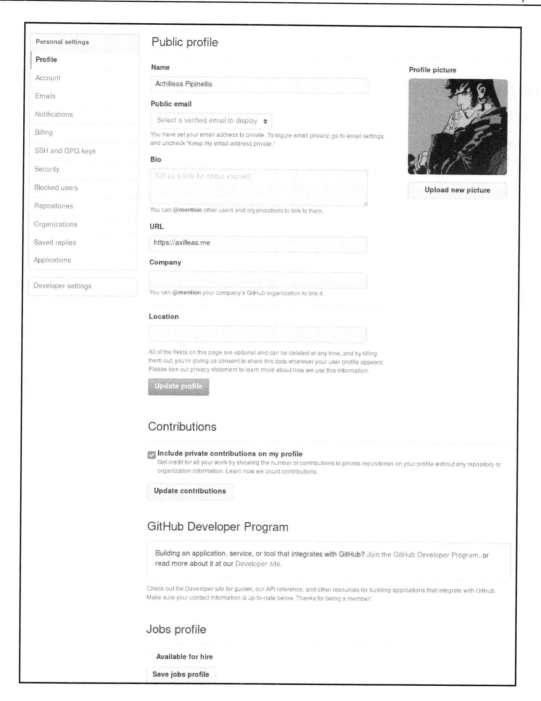

We are going to analyze the most important settings GitHub provides.

Profile

Under **Personal settings**, you can see various options that you can customize to your liking.

The **Profile** settings is where you can fill in your personal information so that people know who you are. Consider it like socialization. After all, GitHub is the Facebook of geeks.

All the profile information is optional to fill in. You can see what this will look like by visiting your username page at `https://github.com/<username>`.

Setting up multiple emails

Every commit is associated with an email address and GitHub uses the email address you set in your local Git configuration to associate commits with your GitHub account. There is no limit to the emails that you can add to your account, but you can have only one primary address. This is where GitHub will send you any notifications and it is this address that will be used when editing and committing files via the web interface.

You can add or remove emails and change the primary address by visiting `https://github.com/settings/emails`. In this area, you can also choose whether or not your primary email will be shown to the public. If you decide to keep your email address private, GitHub will assign an email based on your username: `<username>@users.noreply.github.com`, which will be used whenever you edit files via your browser.

In the following screenshot, you can see what that page looks like when you have multiple emails:

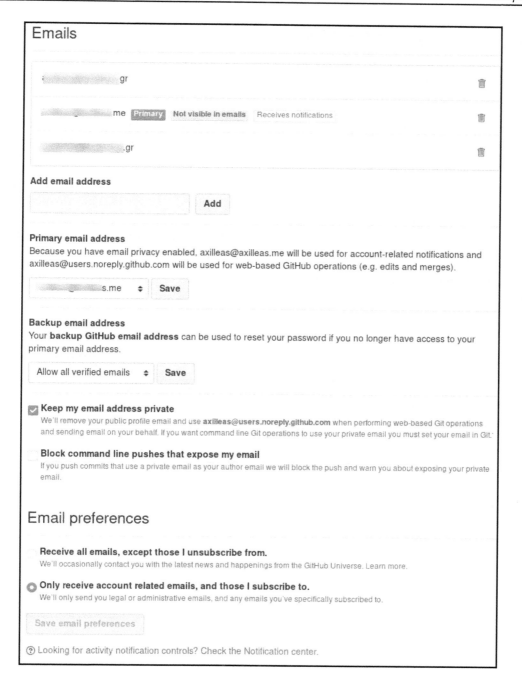

Managing your SSH keys

GitHub provides two ways to authenticate a user when using Git. You can use Git over HTTP or Git over SSH. For a detailed explanation of the Git protocols, visit `https://git-scm.com/book/ch4-1.html`.

When using Git over HTTP, you must provide your username and password each time you make a change, unless you cache your GitHub password in Git. For more details, see the article at `https://help.github.com/articles/caching-your-github-password-in-git/`.

The preferred and more secure way is to use Git over SSH. The concept is that you create a personal unique SSH key pair whose public key you upload to your GitHub profile. You can repeat this process as many times as you wish since GitHub allows you to have multiple SSH keys associated with your account. This way, you can have one key to use with your laptop and a different one with your desktop or your server.

> In order to use Git over SSH, the remote URL of the repository must look like `git@github.com:USERNAME/REPOSITORY.git`.

Under your **Settings** tab, there is the **SSH keys** option. Either navigate through the GitHub UI or go directly to `https://github.com/settings/keys`. When you add an SSH public key, you must give it a **Title** so that you can remember where this key came from. At the **Key** area, you paste the contents of the public key. As you can see, GitHub also provides some useful information such as the fingerprint of the key, when it was added, and when it was last used:

You cannot edit a key. If you want to set a different title, you will have to delete the old key and add it back again.

Setting up two-factor authentication

Setting up two-factor authentication provides an extra layer of security for your account. Using only the password to sign in can prove susceptible to security threats, since the attacker only needs a single piece of information.

This is done by having an extra authentication code generated onto your cell phone or tablet. In the case of a smartphone, you must install an application that can handle the **Time-based One-Time Password** (**TOTP**) technology. If you are looking for an open source application, check `https://github.com/andOTP/andOTP` .

For a list of supported applications, you can read Wikipedia's article at `https://en.wikipedia.org/wiki/Time-based_Onetime_Password_Algorithm#Client_implementations`.

If you do not own a smartphone, GitHub can also send the authentication code with an SMS. Since this involves delivery rates, there is a finite list of supported countries. See if yours is included here: `https://help.github.com/articles/countries-where-sms-authentication-is-supported/#supported-countries-for-sms-authentication`.

You can enable **Two-Factor Authentication** (**2FA**) under the **Security** page. Visit `https://github.com/settings/security` directly and press the **Set up two-factor authentication** button to start setting up 2FA. Pick either one of the methods and follow the on-screen instructions.

After setting up 2FA, if you visit the security page, under your settings, you will see that 2FA is enabled:

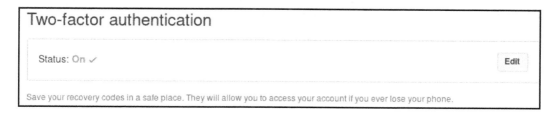

On the **Security** page, make sure to click the link **Save your recovery codes** and follow the on-screen instructions to download and save the recovery codes in a secure place. There are 16 codes that will help you gain access to your account if, for some reason, you lose your cell phone or it gets stolen. Every recovery code can only be used once and you can generate a new batch by clicking on **Generate new recovery codes**. Keep them safe; preferably, store them encrypted in an application such as **KeepassX**.

Now, every time you try to log in to GitHub from a browser for the first time, apart from the usual credentials like username and password, you will be prompted to give the authorization code generated from the application of your smartphone or one of the 16 recovery codes.

Repository settings

There are quite a few settings one can fiddle with at the repository level. To access these settings, search for the wrench icon:

Changing the default branch that appears in a repository's main page

The default branch of a repository's main page is **master**. However, there are times when you want a different branch to be your default, based on one's workflow, as we saw in `Chapter 4`, *Collaboration Using the GitHub Workflow*.

Let's just say, for example, that the **master** branch is where you push code that is considered stable and well-tested, whereas you have a different branch named **develop** that is used for daily pushes and testing new features. Based on this assumption, the **develop** branch gets updated more often than the **master** branch. Practically, you'd want your project to seem active; having a branch that gets updated every day in the front page is much more appealing.

In this case, you can go to the repository's **Settings** > **Branches** page and choose the branch you would like to have as the default from the drop-down list:

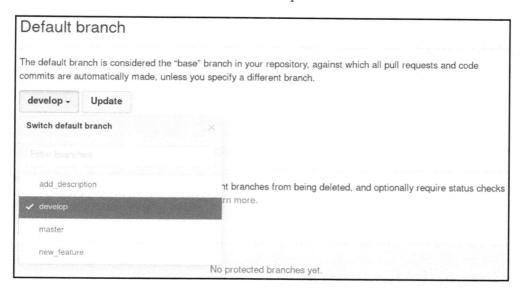

Once selected, click **Update** and accept what GitHub tells you.

> When someone clones the repository for the first time, Git checks out the default branch that is set through the project's settings.

Enabling/disabling the wiki

In Chapter 2, *Using the Wiki and Managing Code Versioning*, we explained in depth why the wiki is a strong asset for a project. There are, however, cases where one does not need a wiki; for example, you might use an external one.

GitHub provides you with three options regarding the visibility of a wiki:

- Enable the wiki and make it public so that everyone has write access (default)
- Enable the wiki, but only owners and collaborators have write access (**Restrict editing to collaborators only**)
- Disable the wiki altogether

The first behavior is the default one. You can find these settings in **Settings** > **Options** under the **Features** block.

Enabling/disabling the issue tracker

Although GitHub's issue tracker is a powerful tool for collaboration and bug reporting, there will be times when you would like to use a different tracker such as Redmine, Jira, or Bugzilla.

In this case, GitHub's issue tracker can be disabled so that you don't have many places to track and lose control. This can be achieved in **Settings** > **Options** under the **Features** block.

 Any created issues are retained, even after you disable the **Issues** feature. Get the tick back and your issue tracker will be the same as before.

Adding collaborators

By adding a collaborator, you are granting push access to the repository. A repository can have many collaborators; there is no limit.

Visit the **Collaborators** tab under settings. Start typing the name of the user and the autocompletion is smart enough to present you with the user you are searching for:

Collaborators	Push access to the repository

This repository doesn't have any collaborators yet. Use the form below to add a collaborator.

Search by username, full name or email address

You'll only be able to find a GitHub user by their email address if they've chosen to list it publicly. Otherwise, use their username instead.

Add collaborator

Transferring ownership – user to organization

Every repository is created under a namespace, be it a user or an organization. In the rare case where you would like to transfer a repository to another user, this can be done in the repository settings. Since this action is considered dangerous, you will find this setting inside a red code block, signifying the importance of the task.

Basically, there are four types of transfer:

- User to user
- User to organization
- Organization to user
- Organization to organization

In order to initialize the transfer, you have to provide the name of the repository and the username/organization of the new owner to confirm:

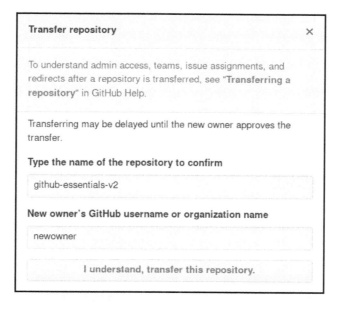

After you hit **I understand, transfer this repository**, an email will be sent to the new owner(s) for confirmation. After they confirm, the procedure will be completed.

Deleting a repository

You can delete a repository along with all its settings by pressing the **Delete this repository** button under **Danger Zone**. Bear in mind that this is a destructive action that will purge your repository, the issue tracker, any pull requests, the wiki, and in general, everything related to it.

After pressing the holocaust button, you will be presented with a modal asking for confirmation. For security reasons, you must provide the repository's name to confirm. In the following screenshot, you can see that unless you provide the right name, the button for deletion will be inactive:

Tips and tricks

Did you know that you can use different email addresses depending on the organization you are member of? Are you aware of how much disk space your repository takes? If no, read the following section, and learn how to perform these actions.

Finding the size of your repositories

If you are curious to know how big your repositories have become, you can visit `https://github.com/settings/repositories` and see it for yourself. Remember that GitHub also counts the size of the `.git` directory, so if you have thousands of commits, the repository's size will be greater than its actual size (by actual size, I mean whatever files you see on GitHub).

For example, the `diaspora` repository at the time of writing this book seems to be **102 MB**:

If I were to remove the `.git` directory, the size would be much smaller. Let's test it by using the following commands:

```
git clone https://github.com/diaspora/diaspora
du -sh diaspora
rm -rf diaspora/.git
du -sh diaspora
```

Removing the `.git` directory gets the size down to almost 14 MB!

Fine-tuning email notifications

If you are a member of many organizations, you may want to use a different email for notifications concerning the repository that a specific organization owns. You can achieve this by going to `https://github.com/settings/notifications`; under **Custom routes**, choose the email you want to receive the notifications.

Summary

By finishing this chapter, you should be ready to fill in the details to build a public profile that is viewable by anyone interested in knowing more about you. Your account is yours and yours only, so it should be secured as much as possible. By now, you should have followed the steps to secure it with 2FA and be a little bit safer.

You have also learned how to configure a repository's settings regarding its default branch and enabling or disabling features such as the issue tracker and the wiki. Another thing to remember is how to add collaborators to your project and how to transfer its ownership if needed.

These were the most important settings to consider, both user and project-related, and you should feel a little bit wiser towards the end.

Other Books You May Enjoy

If you enjoyed this book, you may be interested in these other books by Packt:

Git Version Control Cookbook
Aske Olsson, Rasmus Voss

ISBN: 978-1-78216-845-4

- Understand the Git data model and how you can navigate the database with simple commands
- Learn how you can recover lost commits/files
- Discover how you can force rebase on some branches and use regular Git merge on other branches
- Extract metadata from a Git repository
- Familiarize yourself with Git notes
- Discover how you can work offline with Git
- Debug with Git and use various techniques to find the faulty commit

Git Essentials - Second Edition
Ferdinando Santacroce

ISBN: 978-1-78712-072-3

- Master Git fundamentals
- Be able to "visualize," even with the help of a valid GUI tool
- Write principal commands in a shell
- Figure out the right strategy to run change your daily work with few or no annoyances
- Explore the tools used to migrate to Git from the Subversion versioning system without losing your development history
- Plan new projects and repositories with ease, using online services, or local network resources

Leave a review - let other readers know what you think

Please share your thoughts on this book with others by leaving a review on the site that you bought it from. If you purchased the book from Amazon, please leave us an honest review on this book's Amazon page. This is vital so that other potential readers can see and use your unbiased opinion to make purchasing decisions, we can understand what our customers think about our products, and our authors can see your feedback on the title that they have worked with Packt to create. It will only take a few minutes of your time, but is valuable to other potential customers, our authors, and Packt. Thank you!

Index

B

branches
  and pull request, connecting between 94
  creating, in fork and pull model 95
  creating, in shared repository model 95

C

code versioning
  draft release, creating 53
  files, uploading 53, 54
  managing 46
  pre-release, marking 51, 52
  release, creating 47, 48, 49, 50
  release, editing 50
  tag, pushing from command line 51
community tab 136
continuous integration (CI) 94

G

GitHub Pages
  about 125
  custom domain, used 129
  Jekyll 130
  metadata used, with Jekyll 144, 145
  organization page, creating 126
  project page, creating 126, 127
  theme, selecting for page style 127, 128
  tips and tricks 143
  user page, creating 126
GitHub web editor
  fork and pull model 102, 104
  shared repository model 101
  using 100
global member privileges 64, 66

I

inline comments 105
issue tracker
  benefits 20
  issue creating 22
  issue, assigning to user 23
  issue, creating 20
  labels 24
  milestones 28
  tips and tricks 31

J

Jekyll
  about 130, 133, 134
  installing 130, 131
  used, for customizing page 131, 132, 133

L

labels, issue tracker
  benefits, over UX 25
  colors, setting 25, 27
  name, creating 25, 27
  using, to group issues 27

M

milestones, issue tracker
  adding 30
  code versioning, working with 28
  creating 28
  used, for resolving 30

O

organization
  audit log 85
  creating 61, 64

feed, in dashboard 90
namespace, repository transferring 86, 88
profile 84
roles and repository permission levels 60, 61
security 85
setting 83
teams 86
teams, mentioning 89
third-party access 86
tips and tricks 86
user account, converting 89

P

peer review
  about 105
  process 110, 112, 113
People tab
  about 77, 78
  access levels, managing 78, 80
  members, versus outside collaborators 80, 82
  outside collaborator, demoting 83
pull request
  and branches, connecting between 94
  branch, removing 116
  branch, restoring 116
  Compare & pull request button, using 95, 97
  compare function, using 98, 100
  creating 95
  diff files, downloading 121
  directories creating, web editor used 122
  GitHub web editor, using 100
  global list 121
  issues, closing via commit messages 117, 118
  layout 106, 108
  learning 93
  LICENSE file adding, web editor used 121
  merging 115
  mistakes, correcting 114
  reverting 117
  submitting 95, 104
  task lists 119, 120
  tips and tricks 117
  working with 94

R

repository settings
  about 154
  collaborators, adding 156
  default branch, changing 154
  email notifications, fine-tuning 159
  issue tracker, enabling/disabling 156
  ownership, transferring 157
  repositories size, finding 158
  repository button, deleting 158
  tips and tricks 158
  wiki, enabling/disabling 155
repository
  about 66
  Blame buttons 15, 17
  branches page 14
  commits page 11, 14
  creating 8
  description, changing 19
  exploring 8, 10, 11
  Fork buttons 17
  git branch command, comparison 14
  git log command, comparison 11, 14
  History buttons 16, 17
  Raw buttons 15, 17
  Star buttons 17
  URL changing 19
  Watch buttons 17, 19

S

security tab 85

T

team, joining request
  as owner 73
  as team maintainer 73
  as user 73
team
  creating 67, 68
  discussions 76
  invitation, accepting 71
  joining, request 73
  member permissions 72
  people, inviting 69, 70

repositories, adding 74, 76
selective access, granting to organization
   projects 67
teams tab 86
Time-based One-Time Password (TOTP)
   about 153
   reference link 153
tips and tricks, issue tracker
   keyboard shortcuts, navigating 31
   README file, learning 31

U

user settings
   about 148
   multiple emails, setting up 150
   profile 150
   SSH keys, managing 152
   two-factor authentication, setting up 153
users
   versus organizations 60

V

vulnerable dependencies, security alerts
   reference link 140

W

Web analytics

about 134
code frequency 139
commits tab 138
community profile 136, 137
contributors 135, 136
dependency graph 140
forks tab 142
network 140, 141
pulse 134
traffic tab 142
wiki
   changes, creating in GitHub 56
   changes, pushing to GitHub 56
   cloning 55, 56
   commit history, watching 42, 43, 44, 46
   editing 55
   footer, adding 40, 41, 42
   gollum library, installing 55
   markdown 37, 38, 39
   page, creating 34, 35, 36
   page, deleting 36
   preview, viewing in browser 55, 56
   releases, subscribing via atom feed 54, 55
   sidebar, adding 40, 41, 42
   tips and tricks 54
   used, for documenting project 34
   using 34